INSIDE CENTRAL AMERICA

PANTHEON BOOKS, NEW YORK

Phillip Berryman

INSIDE

CENTRAL

AMERICA

The Essential Facts Past and Present on El Salvador,

Nicaragua, Honduras, Guatemala, and Costa Rica

Copyright © 1985 by Phillip Berryman
All rights reserved under International and Pan-American Copyright Conventions. Published in the United States by Pantheon Books, a division of Random House, Inc., New York, and simultaneously in Canada by Random House of Canada Limited, Toronto.

Library of Congress Cataloging in Publication Data

Berryman, Phillip.
Inside Central America.

Includes index.
1. Central America—Politics and government—
1979–   2. Revolutions—Central America.
3. Central America—Foreign relations—United States.
4. United States—Foreign relations—Central America.
I. Title.
F1439.5.B47 1985   327.730728   84-43002
ISBN 0-394-72943-9 (pbk.)

Book design by Joe Marc Freedman

Manufactured in the United States of America

9876543

CONTENTS

INSIDE CENTRAL AMERICA

INTRODUCTION

The 1970s were not a "Me Decade" in Central America.

People there had suffered decades and even centuries of violent rule by narrow landholding and military elites. In the 1970s, war, earthquakes, floods, and the declining world economy combined to lower most Central Americans' already precarious standard of living. For some time the poor, and others seeking basic changes, put their faith in the existing political process, but they saw that any serious proposals for reform were annulled by fraud or violence. New peasant organizations arose, labor unions became more militant, and church people, students, and others came together in powerful social movements. By 1976 and 1977, these movements were challenging the Somoza dictatorship in Nicaragua and the de facto military dictatorships in El Salvador and Guatemala.

These developments went unnoticed in the United States. For example, between 1972 and 1977, less than one-tenth of 1 percent (0.1%) of television network news coverage was devoted to Central America, a region that President Reagan would later claim stood "at our doorstep." During four of those years no story on El Salvador appeared on any network any night of the year.

By the end of the decade, Americans became aware that Central America was in crisis. In July 1979, the Somoza dictatorship in Nicaragua was overthrown and the Sandinistas set up the first revolutionary government in Latin America since the Cuban Revolution in 1959. The protest movements in El Salvador and Guatemala turned into open insurgencies during the next two years. Since then, Americans have become accustomed to seeing Central America as one of a half-dozen global trouble spots.

Many people intuitively grasped that Central America might become the Vietnam of the 1980s, and many have been indignant over U.S. support for governments that kill their own civilians, or toler-

3

ate their murder. Yet others insist that revolution in Central America must be seen as part of a global superpower struggle and view it as a threat to U.S. interests. Thus there exists a kind of stalemate between human rights and national security considerations.

If some Americans fear another Vietnam, for Central Americans themselves the war is already on. Forty thousand Nicaraguans were killed in the 1978–1979 revolution, and over 2,700 more have died fighting the anti-Sandinista *contras*. Approximately 50,000 Salvadorans have been killed since 1980, and in Guatemala at least 40,000 have been killed for political reasons since the 1960s. Between 1 and 2 million Salvadorans and Guatemalans have been uprooted from their homes and made refugees, many fleeing as far as the United States. The war and the world recession have set Central American economies back a decade or more.

The war in Central America has become more and more Americanized since 1980, when the United States renewed military aid to El Salvador, and 1981, when U.S. advisors arrived. By spring 1984, U.S. Air Force pilots were flying surveillance missions over rebel-held territory in El Salvador, radioing information to Panama. There it was relayed to Washington to be analyzed so that bombing instructions could be sent back to the Salvadoran air force base at Ilopango—all within two hours. The Salvadoran pilot who dropped the bomb was the final link in an American chain. In Nicaragua, the army of anti-Sandinista *contras* (counterrevolutionaries) has been organized and funded by the CIA.

The extent of such U.S. involvement has made Central America a major foreign policy issue. My aim in this book is to present an outline of the main issues and to provide both factual information and a basis for interpretation. A book as short as this one cannot begin to assemble all the relevant data on Central America—the area includes five countries, each with its own history and characteristics*—and U.S. policy there. It must necessarily condense, summarize, and select. What it can do is propose a framework for understanding the present Central American conflicts.

We are not able to view a situation like the one in Central America

---

*The five countries of Central America are Guatemala, El Salvador, Honduras, Nicaragua, and Costa Rica, which have shared a common history and have similar economies. Panama was part of Colombia until 1903, and its economy has always been primarily one of international trade rather than agriculture. Belize was a British colony until it achieved independence in 1981.

with unaided eyes—we are always perceiving it through one set of glasses or another. There are no "pure" facts to be isolated; our interpretations, our feelings, and our world-views are already at work as we select what facts to consider. We can, however, realize that we are wearing such glasses, be critical about them, and even change them, if we choose.

The conventional frameworks for understanding the situation in Central America are either conservative or liberal. The conservative position seems clearer. The starting point is an overall East-West confrontation, and basic policy in Central America is a matter of identifying "enemies" (the Sandinistas and the Salvadoran guerrillas) and "friends" (for example, the present governments of El Salvador, Honduras, and Guatemala and the anti-Sandinista *contras*).

Liberals believe that the problem stems from the resistance of entrenched elites to legitimate pressures for change. The aim should be not to resist change but to channel it constructively, typically by finding the right group or candidate to take charge of the government. Repression and human rights violations are viewed as ultimately be self-defeating.

Although they appear to be at opposite poles, these viewpoints converge much more than their proponents might desire. In practice, each has to adopt elements from the other. It was the liberal Carter administration that began preparing to send El Salvador military aid as early as mid-1979, and later sent the first military advisors. And the conservative Reagan administration has been obliged both to accept the rhetoric of human rights and land reform and to avoid public association with the more blatant manifestations of right-wing violence in Central America. Liberals and conservatives in Congress may engage in a tug of war over particular pieces of legislation, but often they are simply debating over the proper mix of military and economic aid.

While my argument for a fundamental shift in U.S. policy toward Central America may remove me from the liberal-conservative mainstream in the United States, it puts me squarely in the mainstream of what has been advocated by scholars, church people, development workers, and others with firsthand experience in Central America and by Latin American and European political parties and governments as well. Furthermore, I am writing from years of involvement in the region. From 1965 to 1973 I worked as a Catholic priest in Panama City barrios, and from 1976 to 1980 I lived in Guatemala as the American Friends Service Committee representative in Central America. My task there was to interpret developments in the region for concerned groups in the United States. Living under the state terror that reigns in Guatemala, I witnessed firsthand the events I recount in Chapters 1 and 2. During that time many Central Americans I knew were murdered. To cite but one experience: On March 23, 1980, I was leading an ecumenical church delegation to El Salvador and was present at a Sunday Mass during which Archbishop Oscar Romero addressed the nation's soldiers, telling them that God's command "Thou shalt not kill" is higher than any superior's order to kill defenseless peasants. When the archbishop was murdered the next day, I shared people's shock and anguish. The following Sunday I was present in the plaza when his funeral was attacked with bombs and bullets, and roughly 100,000 people were forced to flee.

Through my work, I experienced the step-by-step unfolding of the crisis in Central America long before it was recognized in the United States. Since returning to the United States in mid-1980, I have focused primarily on Central American issues through research, writing, and public speaking.

I do not claim to be unbiased. My bias is in favor of the majority of people in Central America: those who are poor, many of them peasants. My proposals are aimed at bringing them peace and a chance to pursue their lives with some dignity and hope.

Yet I write as an American who seeks to influence U.S. policy in the region. I am not an advocate of any particular group in Central America, although I believe what I say here reflects the aspirations of the majority and of those who are sincerely struggling for their welfare. It is my conviction that what I propose will best serve the real interests of the United States.

Apparently it is not immediately obvious to U.S. policymakers that any valid solution in Central America must focus on the needs of the poor majority. In order to formulate a policy that would represent a bipartisan consensus on Central America, President Reagan in mid-1983 appointed the Kissinger Commission. Ostensibly the commission sought a wide range of viewpoints on the issues. However, on their two lightning-quick trips to Central America, the commission's members met almost exclusively with the region's elites. The commission's list of 104 witnesses who testified at its hearings

in the United States included current and former government officials, military officers and experts, corporation executives and bankers, professors and think-tank scholars. Most had no special expertise on Central America. There was only one scholar whose academic
work had been primarily on Central America. Almost none of those
104 individuals had lived and worked with the poor of Central
America.

Despite the prestige associated with the name of Henry Kissinger,
the commission's report was simply an apology for existing policy
and recommended vastly increased funding. It not only disregarded
the voice of the poor but failed to recognize that the poor themselves
had become organized protagonists in the struggle. Any policy based
on such misconceptions must fail.

The Kissinger Commission report, however, is merely sympto-
matic of a pervasive inability of U.S. policymakers to understand
events in Central America. This book attempts to aid the debate, not
so much by amassing facts as by sharpening the focus.

There is a growing list of critiques and commentaries on U.S.
policy in Central America. Most are motivated by ethical indignation
or by a sense that the country is headed toward one more ill-advised
military intervention. While this book arises out of those same concerns, it puts forward some clear proposals for resolving Central
American conflicts without jeopardizing U.S. security. Hence, it
contributes to the policy debate by making a reasonable calculation
of the pros and cons of different courses of action.

As this book was being written, the United States seemed to be
moving inexorably into a deeper military involvement: the very
premises of existing policy seemed to point toward direct U.S. combat involvement in Nicaragua or El Salvador. Even if there was no
U.S. invasion, all indications were that U.S. efforts to overthrow the
Sandinista government and to defeat the Salvadoran guerrillas would
mean years of bloodshed and destruction, and possibly the disinte-
gration of the social fabric of Central America.

What motivates this book is a hope that such an outcome can be
averted.

Earlier versions of this work were published by the American
Friends Service Committee (AFSC) in 1983 and 1984 under the title
What's Wrong in Central America—and What to Do About It. While
the essential argument of the earlier versions remains the same, this

Pantheon edition has been rewritten and, in fact, doubled in length. I hope it retains the brevity and directness that earlier readers found helpful.

Needless to say, what I present here is my own opinion and not that of the American Friends Service Committee. Nevertheless, I believe it is in the spirit of the AFSC, particularly in its commitment to nonviolence and social justice. While a good deal of this book deals with violence, my aim is not to justify anyone's violence but to find a solid basis for ending all the violence.

The procedure is straightforward. After laying out the historical roots of today's conflicts (Chapter 1) and analyzing the growing U.S. involvement (Chapter 2), I examine the major themes of the Central America debate (Chapter 3) and then project the likely outcomes of present policies (Chapter 4). Finally, I suggest an alternate policy, first by examining whether the United States can deal with revolutionary movements in Central America (Chapter 5), and then by outlining the probable contours of a negotiated approach (Chapter 6).

ONE

ORIGINS OF THE CONFLICT

Since 1979, United States policy in Central America has been based on an assumption that revolutionary movements led by Marxists must represent a serious threat to U.S. interests and security. On this point, the difference between liberals and conservatives is merely one of emphasis or accent.

Such an assumption is not shared by most governments in Western Europe and Latin America. In part, these countries base their positions on their understanding of the origins of the present crisis—that is, the history, both remote and recent, of Central America.

Central American history is all but ignored by conventional U.S. media treatments of the region. With a passing reference to oligarchies or dictatorships, reporters usually take the fall of Somoza in Nicaragua or the October 1979 coup in El Salvador as their starting point. Of course, Americans would regard as preposterous a foreigner's attempt to explain the social and political situation in the United States in the 1980s without referring to Vietnam, Watergate, OPEC, and "stagflation," or without mentioning the struggles of women, blacks, Hispanics, and other groups, as well as the efforts of successive administrations to deal with these events. Yet that is the equivalent of much U.S. commentary on Central America.

In addition, to the extent that U.S. commentators discuss Central American history at all, they tend to focus solely on political history—especially coups, the activities of political parties, and elections. The majority of the people are not considered to be a legitimate political or social force; and so, for example, the struggle in El Salvador is viewed as involving a few thousand guerrillas and the army. The broad masses of the people are assumed to be merely inert or, perhaps, "caught in the crossfire." Given that view, it is not surprising that the major political problem of most Central American countries is seen as finding the "right" group or person to run the government after legitimizing elections. Ordinary people are assumed to be clients of political leaders instead of protagonists in a struggle.

Such an assumption may be valid in societies where there is a consensus, either because ordinary people feel the political system is serving them well, or because the dominant group uses power so effectively that no change seems possible. It is not valid, however, in societies where people have reached the point of organized resistance and struggle—that is, when a revolutionary process is underway.

My aim in this chapter is to tell how that kind of shift occurred in some Central American countries in the 1970s. In order to do so, I must first look at how Central American societies were formed and how the pressure of unresolved problems built up to the point where it could explode in revolution.

AGROEXPORT DESTINY

Central America was born in an act of violence—the conquest of the indigenous people. In the 1520s Spaniards arrived from both north and south and, taking advantage of rivalries among native Indian groups in Guatemala, defeated them and gradually extended that conquest throughout the isthmus. By 1540 the Indians had been largely defeated, although the conquest was not completed in Costa Rica until 1561. As Europeans did elsewhere, the Spaniards inflicted death by weapons and by disease. Some of the decimated native peoples were pushed into remote areas, while others became assimilated through marriage. In Guatemala the Indians retained their identity and still form over half the population. (In the early 1980s the Guatemalan army was battling an insurgency made up largely of Indians.)

Although formally under the Viceroyalty of New Spain (Mexico), the Kingdom of Guatemala, which stretched from Chiapas in southern Mexico to Costa Rica, dealt directly with the Spanish court; it was the administrative center of Central America and its economic and cultural center as well.

Because it soon became clear that there was little gold or silver in the region, the conquerors set up plantations to grow cacao for export markets. Indians were subjugated economically, first by being obliged to pay tribute to Spain, and then by the *repartimiento*, a legal requirement stipulating that each week a quarter of the men of a village had to work for the Spaniards. When production in other regions such as Venezuela made cacao unprofitable, the colonists moved to exporting indigo dyes. This required a great deal of Indian labor. From the conquest to the present, small elites have prospered by controlling the land and commanding a ready supply of very cheap labor.

Because it had no precious metals, Central America remained a backwater during the colonial period. Central Americans did not play an important role in the struggle for independence from Spain. When independence was achieved in 1821, the region briefly came under Mexican control; but in 1823 it became autonomous under the name of the United Provinces of Central America. For almost fifteen years, the United Provinces existed as a political unit, despite sharp Liberal-Conservative battles. Then, in 1837–1838, a series of revolts swept through the isthmus from Guatemala to Costa Rica; and the present five countries became independent nations. The Liberals were eager to promote Enlightenment ideas and to replace Spanish institutions with new ones, often borrowed from Britain or the United States. However, the Liberals offended ordinary people with new forced labor requirements and with laws that enabled large landholders to acquire the peasants' communal lands. Their moves against the Catholic church (the expulsion of some clerics, the suppression of monastic orders, and in general, the ending of church privileges) further disturbed the ordinary people. Conservative dictatorships prevailed during the next generation, and the region became Balkanized.

More important than the political seesaw between Liberals and Conservatives was the introduction of coffee. Production began in Costa Rica in the 1830s. Since colonial times, Costa Rican society had been somewhat less exploitative than that of its neighbors. There was no class of Indians condemned to forced labor. Hence, coffee was produced largely on small- and medium-sized landholdings. By contrast, in the 1870s, when the elites in Guatemala and El Salvador recognized that European industrial growth was creating a rapidly spreading taste for coffee, they enacted decrees making the Indians' communal lands and the Catholic religious orders' lands illegal, so that they could then expropriate them for their own profit.

Around the turn of the century, American entrepreneurs began the banana export operations that soon became the United Fruit and Standard Fruit companies. While coffee production remained in the hands of national elites, the banana companies were foreign enclaves. From the north coast of Honduras, for example, they shipped directly to U.S. ports, from which they also imported what they required. The banana companies acquired vast areas of land there (nearly a million acres in 1914, for example), and made sure that the various Honduran governments were accommodating, but they contributed nothing to the internal development of the country.

INTERVENTION AND DICTATORSHIP

It should not be surprising that in order to maintain an agroexport system that benefitted themselves, the elites systematically applied coercion. In Central America, dictatorship has been the normal method of rule despite the formal apparatus of representative government. During colonial times Indians sometimes rose up against the elites, but these rebellions were local and could be suppressed. That there were further revolts after independence testifies to an enduring sense among Indians and peasants that the social order was unjust.

United States intervention has also played a major role in shaping (or misshaping) Central America. In the 1850s an American adventurer named William Walker and a contingent of "filibusters" (private American citizens who during the nineteenth century fomented revolution in Latin American countries for their own gain) fought on the Liberal side in a Nicaraguan civil war. Walker became head of the army and, in an astounding move, had himself elected president in 1856. The following year he was defeated by an army from neighboring countries. Many in the United States considered Walker to be a hero, and he persisted in his adventures until he was captured and executed in Honduras in 1860.

Although he was a private citizen, many Central Americans saw in Walker a symbol of U.S. expansionism. During the Civil War and the industrial buildup that followed it, there was relatively little U.S. interest in Latin America. But by the turn of the century Americans had become expansionist. Between 1898 and 1920 the United States sent troops to the Caribbean or Central America twenty times. For example, in 1907 the Honduran president, Manuel Bonilla, who had been close to Sam Zemurray, the founder of the United Fruit Company, was overthrown by Miguel Dávila. In 1911 Zemurray launched an invasion from New Orleans to overthrow Dávila. The U.S. Navy intervened, ostensibly to block the invasion. In fact, however, by declaring a neutral zone in Honduras, it prevented Dávila from attacking the invaders. The U.S. consul mediated and appointed a temporary president of Honduras. Rather than face the U.S. Navy, Dávila stepped down, and eight months later Bonilla was elected president.

In 1912 U.S. Marines landed in Nicaragua to protect a president whom the U.S. government had helped install. From that time until 1933 (with one short absence), the marines remained in Nicaragua. Although their numbers were small, they effectively controlled national policy. In 1927, when Augusto César Sandino refused to accept a U.S.-imposed election formula, he found himself involved in a guerrilla war with the marines. Sandino, the son of a landholder and a peasant woman, had worked for American mining and fruit companies in Central America and in Mexico during the revolution there. He began fighting for the Liberal party but gradually came to see that he was struggling against the U.S. domination of his country. Although they pursued him until 1933, the marines did not defeat Sandino. He agreed to a truce when the U.S. forces were withdrawn. In the meantime, the marines had trained the National Guard and put the first Anastasio Somoza in charge. On the night of February 11, 1934, Sandino and two of his aides were picked up by National Guardsmen, taken out to a field, and shot down. They were later buried under the airport runway. Hundreds of Sandino's followers were then murdered. Anastasio Somoza went on to establish a dictatorship that was to last forty-five years.

As the Great Depression brought plummeting coffee prices and widespread unemployment, the Central American oligarchies responded to growing unrest with repression. Dictators ruled everywhere but Costa Rica. In El Salvador, growing conflict led to a peasant (largely Indian) uprising in January 1932. The uprising was put down easily and its leaders, including Agustín Farabundo Martí, a communist, were captured and killed. However, for good measure, the dictator, Maximiliano Hernández Martínez, ordered troops to keep killing peasants. The resulting slaughter of 30,000 peasants was seared into the memories of Salvadorans. Postcards showing one of the Indian leaders executed by hanging were sold in San Salvador.

After the massacre, Indians in El Salvador stopped wearing traditional garb and Indian identity virtually disappeared.

Hernández Martínez represented the coffee growers and resisted efforts at modernization. He dabbled in the occult and freely indulged his own bizarre ideas. For example, during a measles epidemic, he ordered street lamps to be covered with colored cellophane to purify the air. In 1944 he was overthrown by a civilian movement, but the coffee oligarchy and the conservative military soon reasserted control.

That same year in Guatemala a largely middle-class revolt threw out the dictator Jorge Ubico. For the next ten years Guatemala experienced democracy and underwent a series of reforms. However, the Eisenhower administration regarded the government of Jacobo Arbenz as communist controlled. Moreover, in 1953 the government began a land reform program in which over a thousand estates were expropriated and land distributed to over 100,000 families in a year and a half. The Arbenz government applied the reform to the United Fruit Company, the largest landholder in the country, offering to pay for the land at the value the company had been declaring for tax purposes (which was a fraction of its real worth). Cold War ideology and economic interests went hand in hand, since John Foster Dulles, the U.S. secretary of state, was also a member of the law firm that served United Fruit.

The United States sought to isolate Guatemala diplomatically, and the CIA undermined the government with such covert actions as flying over Indian villages and dropping copies of an anticommunist pastoral letter written by Archbishop Rossell of Guatemala City. When the CIA bombed Guatemala City and the Guatemalan army, already undermined by the CIA, refused to support him, Arbenz resigned. The new president, Carlos Castillo Armas, was flown in on a U.S. embassy plane. The wealthy were given back their land, union leaders and others were killed or jailed (the "liberating force" used lists supplied by the U.S. embassy), and Guatemalans began to experience the long night of murder and repression under army domination that continues to this day.

For Central Americans these developments—the Somoza dictatorship, the 1932 massacre in El Salvador, and the CIA overthrow of the Arbenz government—were severe traumas. Real power remained concentrated in the hands of small rich landholding elites, backed up by the military, who were willing to imprison, torture, and murder opponents. Governments may have fluctuated between electoral democracy and military dictatorship, but no political movement was able to seriously threaten the power of the elites. Moreover, those elites could count on the support of the United States. Hence, for decades they could afford to ignore the needs of the majority and suppress occasional protest.

MODERNIZATION AND CRISIS

In the conventional view, the "crisis" in Central America erupted in the late 1970s and was the result either of an economic decline brought about by the world recession (according to liberals) or of Marxist subversion (according to conservatives). In the experience of Central Americans, however, both the crisis and people's struggle to deal with it occurred much earlier. The crisis was primarily a result of the way the development of the last few decades has affected ordinary people.

Central America was slow to modernize, even by Latin American standards. The coffee elites had little incentive to innovate, since their profits enabled them to import expensive automobiles and other luxury goods, to send their children abroad for study, and to travel themselves. Nevertheless, by the 1940s there was a growing sentiment for "modernization." Modernizers believed that their countries should both move away from an almost total dependence on coffee and export other corps and begin to industrialize in order to manufacture the products that were being imported. The civilian movements that overthrew the personal dictatorships in El Salvador and Guatemala in 1944 were motivated partly by a sense that Hernández Martínez and Ubico stood in the way of modernization. In Nicaragua the Somozas themselves took up modernization.

This internal impulse for modernization was reinforced by two international trends. The first push toward development began in the 1950s and was manifested in the World Bank and in United Nations programs around the world. The second occurred in the 1960s with the Alliance for Progress, which the United States launched in response to the shock of the Cuban Revolution. Various approaches to development were taken: loans for large infrastructure projects (such as roads, dams, or ports), aid for institution-building (for example, U.S. experts working within a Central American government to develop health or educational systems), and technical assistance (such as introducing new agricultural methods). In the later phases there was more stress, at least in rhetoric, on grassroots development at the village level.

Development and modernization did not seriously threaten the elites' hold over Central American societies. For example, one of the stated aims of the Alliance for Progress was to carry out land reforms; however, the existing governments were consistently unwilling, or unable, to challenge the power of the large landholders.

From the 1940s onward, the landholding elites moved into sugar, cotton, and beef. Such enterprises require large tracts of low, flat land, which wealthy landowners often took directly from the peasants who were farming it. In any case, the land available to peasants for the production of basic foods such as corn and beans declined. For example, in Guatemala, between 1950 and 1973 agroexport acreage was increasing at the rate of 6.5 percent a year, while land for food production increased at a rate of only 1.7 percent to 2 percent. At the same time, the population was growing at a rate of 3 percent a year. The amount of land available to peasants shrank dramatically. Between 1955 and 1975, the size of an average plot for a Guatemalan Indian family was cut in half. Similar trends occurred in El Salvador and Nicaragua.

During the 1960s, private, government, and international development agencies sought to aid peasants through cooperatives, new farming techniques, and the introduction of chemical fertilizers and pesticides. For a time, the increased yields offset the impact of the dwindling amount of available land. However, these developments were only improvements. They did not bring basic change. Those who had more land, of course, benefitted proportionately. Those with no land saw no gain.

Indeed, there were growing numbers of "landless peasants." Traditionally some workers and their families had lived on plantation property and had been allowed to farm small plots for their own consumption in return for their labor. However, many plantation owners found it easier to end these arrangements and put all their lands into agroexport production. Since the labor supply was large, it was easier to have all the work done for cash by local and migratory labor.

In El Salvador, the landless portion of the rural population increased from 11 percent in 1961 to 40 percent by 1975. Some of these people had sharecropping arrangements—that is, they worked on someone else's land according to prior agreement, such as splitting the product 50/50. As the numbers of landless peasants grew, and in the absence of any unionization (rural unions are illegal in El Salvador), they had even less bargaining power with the plantation managers. During the mid- to late-1970s, the normal pay for agricultural labor (such as cutting a ton of sugar cane under a grueling tropical sun) was around $1.50 a day.

In short, while agricultural modernization brought a diversification and expansion of agroexports and profits for the elites, it brought a decline in the amount of peasant-owned land and in basic food production. Modernization actually worsened conditions for rural people.

As far back as the early 1950s, the notion of a "common market" for Central America seemed logical. Individually these five countries offered no significant market for industrialization, but their combined population lay somewhere between that of Peru and that of Colombia.

When the Central American Common Market was launched in 1960, industrial trade between the countries was minimal. Within a dozen years, however, it had become a significant part of each country's economy and had stimulated the formation or expansion of hundreds of factories for food processing, clothing, shoes, pharmaceuticals, plastics, agricultural chemicals, and household items. The Common Market was Central America's version of the "import substitution" strategy other Latin American countries had employed two or three decades before. Local firms began to manufacture goods that had previously been imported. However, the new industries were far less "Central American" than originally planned. In fact, most were extensions of foreign—largely United States—companies. The small middle classes could now breakfast on Tang, Kellogg's Corn Flakes, or pancakes with Log Cabin syrup; but the Common Market had little to offer the majority of the people, who lived at near-subsistence levels. Although the original planners intended the industries to be spread evenly among the five countries, Guatemala and El Salvador had a head start on infrastructure and they therefore attracted a disproportionate share of new investment. Most importantly, these industries were capital intensive and did little to absorb the labor of peasants forced off the land.

Thus modernization did take place. During the 1960s and into the 1970s, expansion into new crops and industrialization led to an average growth rate of almost 6 percent. Yet at the same time, real living conditions for many people declined. Rural people had less land and the numbers of landless grew. Yet the cities could not provide work for the displaced population. The buying power of workers' wages declined, especially during the 1970s. There are indications that average calorie intake actually declined for many people.

The 1969 war between Honduras and El Salvador was one manifestation of this crisis. Responding to pressures from organized peasants, the Honduran government decided to initiate a land reform program. In order to make land available, it began to expel Salvadoran peasants, some of whom had lived in Honduras for decades. The Salvadoran elites, fearing the impact of tens, or even hundreds, of thousands of peasants in their densely crowded country, began to drum up war fever. In June the Salvadoran army invaded Honduras. In retaliation, the Honduran air force bombed San Salvador. After some 4,000 people, mainly Honduran peasants, had lost their lives, a cease-fire and truce were arranged. Once the two countries had broken relations, there were strong forces against normalizing them. Honduras refused to allow Salvadoran vehicles or goods to cross its territory. Thus, Salvadoran industries could no longer export to Honduras, and could export to Nicaragua and Costa Rica only by boat, across the Gulf of Fonseca. Honduran and other industrialists were quite content to be free from Salvadoran competition.

What the U.S. media called the "Soccer War" (because it had been partly triggered by incidents at soccer games between the two countries) was in fact a product of underlying social tensions and the unwillingness of the ruling oligarchies and militaries to accept change, especially in land tenure.

Central American elites are true oligarchies—small groups that hold the essential power, both economic and political. For example, in Guatemala the top 2 percent of the population receives 25 percent of the income, while the bottom 50 percent receives from 10 to 15 percent. Averaging this last figure at 12.5 percent, the top 2 percent has *fifty times* the per capita income of the bottom half of the population.

These income distribution figures simply reflect the fact that a very small group of people own, and benefit from, the country's productive wealth. Although there are 30,000 coffee producers in Guatemala, 55 percent of the coffee is produced on around 300 plantations and one-third of it on just 79; that is, a relatively small group of families holds the bulk of the nation's principal export. Since these same people own cotton and sugar plantations and beef ranches, as well as the country's businesses and industries, they form a relatively compact and socially isolated group. In order to safeguard and further their interests, from the 1950s onward, they set up business and trade organizations such as coffee producers' associations. These associations were unified into chambers (such as the Chamber of Agriculture); these in turn were combined into single organizations representing the "private sector" in each country. They are known by their acronyms: COSEP in Nicaragua, ANEP in El Salvador, and CACIF in Guatemala.

For decades it has been said that "Fourteen Families" run El Salvador—one for each province of the country. While it may not be literally true that fourteen families run a country by themselves, oligarchies are a reality throughout Central America and they have organized themselves to insure that their fundamental interests are safeguarded. They maintain tight-knit, closed social circles that set them apart from the majority of their own fellow citizens. Many are more familiar with the shopping centers of London or Miami than with the rural areas of their own countries.

Modernization did not threaten the oligarchies. In fact, they were the ones who shaped it and benefitted from it. They became associates of the U.S. companies that arrived to take advantage of the Common Market, and at the same time they effectively vetoed U.S. proposals for land reform.

This is a crucial point for understanding the present crisis. In the conventional view, modernization brought impressive growth—which, admittedly, was not shared equitably; but the economic crisis is attributable primarily to petroleum price increases and the world recession that brought declining prices for the region's exports. However, closer examination reveals that the crisis is largely a product of the development model that was used to achieve modernization. It was no accident that people's real living conditions declined while growth remained high—the same kind of development produced both results.

Defining the economic origin of the crisis is not just a scholarly quibble. The Kissinger Commission, for example, reflecting the conventional view, recommended programs that would amount to a rerun of the Alliance for Progress. There is no reason to believe, however, that the kind of economic development pursued in the 1960s, which produced the crisis, can help to resolve it in the 1980s. What is required is a new model of development.

THE RISE OF
MILITANT OPPOSITION

During the 1970s the crisis in Central America generated broad, organized opposition movements. These movements were rooted in a long history of struggle. During colonial times and throughout the last century, there were periodic peasant and Indian uprisings. In the 1920s and 1930s Augusto César Sandino resisted the U.S. Marine occupation of Nicaragua, and Agustín Farabundo Martí's labor organizing in El Salvador led to the uprising of 1932 and the disastrous massacre. Dictatorships in El Salvador and Guatemala were overthrown in 1944 by movements that were largely nonviolent and led by the emerging middle classes. In 1954 Honduran workers carried out a successful strike against the American banana companies that was a watershed in Honduran history: it signaled the rise of organized peasant movements and labor unions and convinced the banana companies they could no longer operate with their accustomed highhandedness in Honduras.

Nicaraguans periodically fought to overthrow the Somoza dictatorship. In 1961 a small group formed the Sandinista National Liberation Front (FSLN). For fifteen years, however, the FSLN remained a small band, suffering many serious defeats and often seemingly on the edge of extinction.

During the 1960s there arose in Guatemala a complex, largely Marxist, guerrilla movement. Its military operations were confined to one area and it never numbered more than 300 combatants; but from 1966 to 1968 the Guatemalan army—with U.S. aid, training, and advisors—killed an estimated 6,000 to 8,000 people in order to stamp it out. U.S. military aid and training was a key element in shaping the Guatemalan Army.

Although the guerrillas had been defeated by 1970, the Guatemalan army and right-wing political parties judged that subversion was still a threat and therefore extended death-squad activities to Guatemala City. Every year during the 1970s, several hundred civil-

ians—peasants, union leaders, and others perceived as organizers—
were murdered.

Guerrilla movements were formed in El Salvador in 1970, but they
engaged in very few actions until much later in the decade.

The guerrilla movements in Guatemala, Nicaragua, and El Salvador had much in common. Although they were Marxist, they were
not led by communist parties—that is, parties linked to Moscow. In
fact, the existing communist parties in those countries repeatedly
denounced the guerrilla organizations as "adventurist." There were
splits and factions among the guerrillas in each country. In no case
were they a major threat to the regimes until the late 1970s. What
made them a threat was the rise of the "popular organizations,"
which were broad-based and militant, but nonviolent in their
methods.

For the sake of clarity, I will consider in some detail how these
organizations developed in El Salvador, and then draw brief parallels
to Nicaragua and Guatemala.

For a time the 1960s seemed promising to Salvadoran peasants.
With help from the church, private aid agencies, the Peace Corps,
and the Christian Democratic party, they formed cooperatives and
learned new farming techniques. In their organizations they acquired leadership skills and gained confidence in dealing with government authorities. The Christian Democratic party seemed to embody a new ideology that promised change, and its leaders seemed
to be honest. The United States itself appeared to be on the side of
significant reform.

As already noted, these efforts brought little real improvement in
living standards. In fact, repression actually increased. The Alliance
for Progress, conceived as a response to the Cuban Revolution, had
a counterinsurgency component. General José Medrano, then a senior officer of the Salvadoran National Guard and the army general
staff, in close collaboration with the United States, was the major
founder of the paramilitary organization ORDEN (Democratic Nationalist Organization), and ANSESAL (National Security Agency).
Much later Medrano told a reporter that these agencies "grew out of
the State Department, the CIA, and the Green Berets during the time
of Kennedy. . . . We organized ORDEN, ANSESAL, and counterinsurgency courses, and we bought special arms—G3 automatic rifles—
to detain the communist movement." Labor and peasant leaders,
schoolteachers, and church people came under extensive surveil-

lance and occasionally suffered violence. ORDEN and ANSESAL were the seedbeds of the death squads that emerged later.

Yet many people still hoped that electoral politics could provide a channel for peaceful but real change. In the 1972 election, a reform coalition made up of the Christian Democrats and two other parties ran against the official party. The reform presidential candidate was José Napoleón Duarte, who had served two terms as mayor of San Salvador. Guillermo Ungo was his running mate. All commentators agree that the reform coalition received a majority of the votes but was defrauded of the election by the government and the army. A month later, a group of officers attempted a coup in order to recognize the Duarte victory. The coup was suppressed (with the help of bombing from Guatemala and Nicaragua). At that point, many people began to believe that popular elections in El Salvador were irrelevant in the face of oligarchical and military power.

A major catalyst for change was, surprisingly, the Catholic church, traditionally one of the props of the status quo. At Vatican Council II (1962–1965), the Catholic hierarchy had endorsed major changes in church practice, such as replacing the Latin Mass with worship in the people's own language. Whereas previously the church's business had seemed to be primarily a matter of saving souls, it now became common to regard social justice and human development as related to the Kingdom of God.

The ferment of the 1960s was already affecting the church in Latin America when the Catholic bishops met at Medellín, Colombia, in 1968 to apply Vatican II to their continent. The resulting Medellín documents were a kind of Magna Carta that stimulated church people to examine critically their societies and their own pastoral work. Many priests and sisters sought to draw closer to ordinary people, often leaving relative comfort to live among the poor. They became convinced that they must enter into dialogue with the people—not only to teach and catechize, but to learn from them, even to be "evangelized by the poor." Out of this experience there developed a new model of church pastoral work called *comunidades eclesiales de base*, or "grassroots Christian communities." These were small groups of people at the village or barrio level who met under their own lay leadership for Bible reading and study, worship, and self-help. Gradually, the focus of pastoral work shifted from the parish church to these local communities.

There people learned a new way of reading the Bible and understanding their faith, by relating it to what was happening around them. For example, if, as the book of Genesis teaches, human beings have been created in God's image, they have a great dignity; hence, to torture another human being is to disfigure God's image. If the Lord gave the Earth to Adam and Eve, he meant it for all—not just a few plantation owners. By the same token, if God set Adam over the Earth to "subdue" it, creation is not something fixed forever; rather it is the task of human beings to develop it. Similarly, Jesus' statement "The poor you have always with you" should not be used to legitimize an exploitive economic system. Indeed, Jesus' whole message takes on liberating force, and he is seen to preach a God who stands with the poor. The persecution and execution he endured are similar to what happens today to those who struggle for justice, while his resurrection was God's vindication of his life as well as of the lives of those who struggle today.

These and similar interpretations became the foundation of what has come to be called "liberation theology," a way of understanding Christian belief, Christian life, and the mission of the church from the side of the poor and their demand for justice.

In El Salvador the new ideas began to be implemented in 1969. Grassroots Christian communities quickly became the predominant model of church pastoral work in a large part of rural El Salvador, in areas that have been battle sites in recent years, including Suchitoto, Aguilares, San Martín, Guazapa, Arcatao, and Zacatecoluca.

The grassroots Christian communities served primarily to raise consciousness. Within them, people developed both a critical view of the status quo and a motivation to work together. Sooner or later, they would conclude that they needed to be organized.

What kind of organization did they need? Experiences such as the 1972 election fraud had convinced many that political parties, even when they were not mere instruments of the military or the oligarchy, simply had no power to propose and effect fundamental change. Hence, those who worked at organizing the new popular organizations envisioned them not as vehicles for electoral politics but rather as instruments through which the broad masses of the people, especially peasants, could bring direct pressure to bear on the power structure.

During the early 1970s, FECCAS (Federation of Christian Peasants of El Salvador) began to spread rapidly in the rural area north of San Salvador. In fact, FECCAS was an existing organization that had been started by the Christian Democrats in the 1960s. Organizers helped the peasants turn it into a militant means whereby they could pressure for their rights.

In November 1974 an event occurred in the center of the country—in the village of La Cayetana, San Vicente province—that was to become a landmark for many. A Christian community occupied a parcel of idle land, hoping to persuade the owner to rent it out. Instead, government troops attacked the peasants, killing six and arresting twenty-six. Thirteen of these were never seen again—they were among the first of the "disappeared." In response, peasants in that area formed another organization, the UTC (Union of Rural Workers), which then spread through many areas. FECCAS and UTC subsequently joined forces.

During this same period, peasant leaders, church workers, university people, labor leaders, and others met several times, eventually forming a coalition called FAPU (United Popular Action Front).

The pace of events quickened in 1975. In July, government troops opened fire on a protest demonstration in San Salvador organized by university students. The troops trapped the demonstrators on a bridge. Some were killed in the crossfire and some jumped off the bridge to their death. Others were carried away in ambulances and were never seen again. With the cooperation of some priests and sisters, the demonstrators organized a funeral celebration and then occupied the cathedral for several days.

Although they were united in their opposition to the military and the government, the new organizations began to feud among themselves even in the cathedral. Ideological differences led one large group, including FECCAS, to split from FAPU and form the Revolutionary People's Bloc. Their own tensions notwithstanding, the popular organizations were now a part of the national political scene.

Up to this point, the guerrilla organizations—the ERP (People's Revolutionary Army) and the FPL (Popular Liberation Forces)—that had been started in 1970 had scarcely carried out any actions. They were also feuding. One of these feuds led to the "trial" and "execution" of ERP member and poet Roque Dalton, and then to a split and the formation of a new guerrilla group, the RN (National Resistance).

What was the relationship between the guerrilla groups and the popular organizations? It seems quite probable that from an early point, some of the organizers may have been connected to the guerrilla groups, and that guerrilla groups did political work with these organizations as part of a larger strategy. However, the popular organizations were a genuine expression of the peasants' and other poor people's desire for political and social change. Their leaders were peasants, and their means of struggle—demonstrations and strikes—were nonviolent.

In 1976, the government, headed by General Arturo Molina, proposed a very mild land reform that was scheduled to begin in two of the country's fourteen provinces. It was really a kind of pilot project for 12,000 peasant families in a country in which 112,000 families had no land and another 236,000 families had very small holdings. Plantation owners were to be reimbursed partly with bonds that could be reinvested in industry. A few farsighted military officers and businesspeople hoped that such a pilot project could lead to a "Taiwan model" of development. Peasants would acquire land while plantation owners would evolve into industrialists. These proponents claimed the pilot project would be an "insurance policy for our grandchildren" (presumably against another 1932-style peasant uprising). However, the landholders and most of the private sector did not appreciate such foresight, and they reacted vigorously, uniting around the defense minister, General Humberto Romero. By October the government had backed down, and Romero had become the "official" candidate for the upcoming presidential elections.

Flush with a sense of triumph, the oligarchy and security forces unleashed an attack on the popular organizations and on the church, which they regarded as being responsible for growing peasant militancy. Starting in January 1977, several priests were arrested and tortured, and several were expelled. Through electoral fraud, the government and military guaranteed the victory of General Romero over the opposition coalition (which had chosen a retired colonel as candidate in the hope of reassuring the military). The opposition (primarily Christian Democrats and Social Democrats) then held a week-long vigil in a plaza in downtown San Salvador. On February 28, government troops attacked the demonstrators, killing an estimated 100 people (blood had to be fire-hosed off the streets).

On March 12, Rutilio Grande, a fifty-year-old Jesuit and the pastor of Aguilares, was machine-gunned while driving through canefields to say Mass. His killers may have thought they were retaliating for the kidnapping and killing of the head of the government tourist agency. That action, however, was the work of ERP guerrillas. Grande had had no connection with guerrilla groups; furthermore, he had insisted that the church remain independent of groups like FECCAS (while at the same time defending the people's right to organize). In May another priest was killed in San Salvador—again, as a kind of retaliation after the FPL guerrillas had kidnapped the foreign minister and then killed him when President Molina refused to free political prisoners in exchange for his release. With helicopters, armored vehicles, and thousands of troops, the army carried out a major military sweep of the Aguilares area, rounding up peasants, arresting hundreds, and killing fifty or more. When they came to the town of Aguilares, they took over the church, turning it into a barracks. Finally, in June, the White Warriors' Union, a paramilitary organization, ordered all Jesuits to leave the country. If they refused, they would be murdered one by one. The Jesuits stayed, and the bizarre character of the threat finally drew international attention to El Salvador.

This violence was the power structure's reaction to organized peasant militancy. By means of popular organizations, the peasants had presented their demands, such as pay hikes for field workers and standards for the food given them on plantations. To press these demands, they had organized strikes and demonstrations, often in the streets of San Salvador. They had been organized at both the village and national levels, and that had given them strength. The power structure correctly saw them as a threat and responded with violence.

This violence in early 1977, and especially the postelection massacre, was a watershed. Many were now convinced that no change could come through the existing political system. The new mass organizations grew rapidly and put increasing pressure on the government. Labor unions became involved, as did slum dwellers, university students, teachers, and others. In order to give an appearance of legality to arbitrary repression, President Romero decreed a sweeping "Law of Public Order and Security." During 1978, church human rights groups found that 1,063 people had been arrested for political reasons, 147 had been killed by security forces, and another 23 had disappeared after arrest.

While the overwhelming majority of acts of violence so far had been committed by official troops and ORDEN, the counterinsurgency paramilitary organization established in the 1960s, guerrilla groups now began to carry out a number of kidnappings, demanding ransom monies and sometimes the release of political prisoners. At one point in early 1979, a Salvadoran coffee grower, two English businessmen, and a Japanese industrialist were all being held by guerrilla groups. The Japanese was killed when ransom demands were not met.

Despite the harsh repression, opposition militancy continued to grow, while the Romero government had no clear program and seemed increasingly unable to govern.

In Guatemala similar developments were taking place. The repression that began in response to guerrilla movements in the 1960s had never ceased. Throughout the 1970s hundreds of people a year were killed for political reasons, very often peasants whose tortured and mutilated bodies were dumped on roadsides. Nevertheless, labor unions became more active after the 1976 earthquake, partly because inflation was lowering real income and also because the government itself seemed somewhat constrained by the presence of international aid agencies. Indians in the highlands organized in order to defend themselves against army aggression. As in El Salvador, the church played an important role in consciousness-raising. Although the rate of killing soon rose—Guatemalan newspapers gave accounts of 979 killings or disappearances during 1978—militant organizations continued their struggle.

In El Salvador and Guatemala during the 1970s, peasants, workers, students, and slum dwellers became a powerful force, sometimes through existing organizations such as labor unions, and sometimes through new organizations or coalitions. Their militant style was expressed in mass demonstrations, strikes, and takeovers of buildings or property. Although these actions were aggressive, they were essentially nonviolent. These popular organizations became the major political force, even though they largely by-passed the existing electoral process. Many commentators today seem scarcely aware of them. The Kissinger Commission report, for example, simply ignores these popular struggles during the 1970s.

Since their language and analysis were Marxist, and since they eventually became linked to guerrilla groups, it seems reasonable to assume that from early on some people connected with guerrilla organizations were also working politically with the popular organizations. However, these organizations were genuine expressions of the aspirations of peasants and workers, and their means of struggle were nonviolent, despite the violence used against them. Oscar Arnulfo Romero, the archbishop of San Salvador, certainly considered them legitimate. In 1978 he published a major pastoral letter called "The Church and the Popular Organizations." His central point was that people should not regard the church and a political organization as the same thing. At the village level, people apparently experienced such overlap or continuity between the grassroots Christian community and peasant organizations like FECCAS that it was easy to confuse the two. While advising them to maintain the distinction, Romero defended the legitimacy of these organizations, and did so until he was murdered in 1980.

By the end of the 1970s, several hundred thousand people in El Salvador (out of a population of less than five million) had become involved in popular organizations. These mass organizations were political but they were not oriented toward elections. As their members saw it, traditional politicians came to the people only at election time. Political parties did not provide any way for them to defend their rights and promote their interests. The popular organizations, by contrast, were continually active, seeking to dramatize the situation of the people and bring pressure to bear through strikes, demonstrations, and occupations of public buildings. They were organized from the village up, although they also had a national structure.

Since 1979 these organizations have become the primary target of the so-called death squads (see Chapters 2 and 3), and that is the greatest sign of their strength and importance.

Today many advocate "political" solutions in Central America. What they often fail to see is that the rise of the popular organizations was itself a thoroughly political process, even though it took place largely outside the channels of existing political parties. It was the violent repression unleashed against these organizations that drove many of their members to become guerrilla combatants. Any "political" solution which ignores that earlier history is not likely to succeed.

A REVOLUTION TAKES POWER

Revolutions usually occur by surprise. Only by hindsight can scholars and theorists explain why they were "inevitable." Certainly in the mid-1970s neither outside experts nor Central Americans themselves would have predicted what was to happen. Indeed, up to early 1978, El Salvador showed more unrest than Nicaragua.

Yet as far back as the 1960s and early 1970s Nicaraguan students and others became militant over particular issues. Teachers went on strike and others occupied the cathedral in Managua to demand justice for political prisoners. Some of these prisoners held a hunger strike in 1972. After the December 1972 earthquake, when Somoza and his associates engaged in cynical and gross profiteering from international aid, he began to lose his legitimacy among the middle and upper classes. In December 1974 the Sandinistas staged a daring hostage operation, forcing Somoza to release some political prisoners as well as pay a ransom, thus momentarily making him seem vulnerable. His response was to unleash the National Guard on the peasants in a "counterinsurgency" campaign. Several hundred peasants thought to be Sandinista collaborators were killed. With his greed, Somoza had alienated large sectors of the business community, and hence during the 1970s middle- and upper-class opposition to his dictatorship grew. Opposition political parties could challenge Somoza's legitimacy, but they could not come close to defeating him politically since he arbitrarily determined the rules of the game. The position of the Catholic hierarchy closely paralleled those of the business sector and opposition parties. In mid-1977, Somoza suffered a heart attack, which again made him seem vulnerable, even after he had recovered. The Sandinistas moved to the offensive in October 1977.

The January 1978 murder of Pedro Joaquín Chamorro, editor of the opposition newspaper *La Prensa*, sparked a sudden mass opposition. Fifty thousand people took to the streets. Business and labor cooperated in a general work stoppage. Next, the people of Monimbo, a barrio of the town of Masaya, rose in rebellion, standing off Somoza's helicopters, tanks, and bazookas with primitive homemade weapons. From that time on, the struggle became continuous, and the Somoza regime increasingly lost legitimacy both in Nicaragua and abroad.

When the Sandinistas staged an impressive action in August 1978, taking 2,000 government employees hostage, people in five provincial cities rose up. Somoza was able to quell these uprisings only by bombing. The National Guard's brutality drove people, especially the young, over to the Sandinistas. The United States sought to find a transition formula whereby Somoza would be persuaded to step down without allowing the Sandinistas to assume control of the government, but its slowness and Somoza's stubbornness prevented any such solution.

Finally, in June 1979, the Sandinistas launched a final offensive. With help from guerrillas, ordinary Nicaraguans took over their towns and cities, setting up barricades and aiding combatants. Diplomatically isolated and without U.S. support, Somoza eventually agreed to step down. The Sandinistas accepted a transition formula; but the provisional president, Francisco Urcuyo, surprisingly announced his intention to remain in office. At that point, the National Guard fell apart, and the Sandinistas triumphantly entered Managua.

This sequence of events is well known. However, it is often asserted that Somoza was overthrown by an alliance between the "moderate opposition" and the Sandinistas, who then "betrayed" the revolution. Such an understanding reflects an elitist perspective. It was neither the moderates nor the Sandinistas who overthrew the dictatorship—it was the majority of the Nicaraguan people. It was they who set up the barricades, hid Sandinista combatants, distributed food, and performed other tasks. It was they who suffered more than 40,000 deaths. Virtually no moderates were killed—except those who became Sandinista combatants.

The middle- and upper-class moderates played an important role because they lent respectability to the anti-Somoza struggle and aided with their money and resources. The Sandinistas, of course, battled Somoza's National Guard. But the Nicaraguan revolution can be understood only as a revolution—that is, as a convulsive social transformation that involved vast sectors of the population.

It was clear from the outset that the Sandinistas' aim was not merely to overthrow the Somoza dictatorship but to bring about profound structural changes in Nicaraguan society. These would inevitably affect the lives of the privileged, even those who had opposed Somoza. Opposition to the Sandinistas was bound to arise, although it was low-keyed during the first few months of the postvictory honeymoon.

To the surprise of practically all observers, in July 1979 the first revolutionary government in Latin America since the 1959 Cuban Revolution had appeared in Nicaragua, and revolutionary struggles were plainly underway in both El Salvador and Guatemala.

TWO

CONFRONTING REVOLUTION: STEP-BY-STEP

The United States originated in an act of revolt—indeed, the Declaration of Independence declares a right to revolution. Nevertheless, present-day Americans find it hard to really understand revolutions like those occurring in Central America.

Perhaps that is because the American Revolution took place long ago against a far-off king. More important, the experience of Central Americans seems as remote to people in the United States as that of the colonists who rebelled against George III. Yet any approach to Central American policy must squarely face the fact that revolutions in the region are underway.

The events in Central America described in the previous chapter share many characteristics with other revolutions in our century, from Mexico and Russia to Vietnam and Zimbabwe. Generalizing somewhat, we may say that revolutions tend to occur when an old social structure breaks down, often when peasants are rapidly losing their land and their traditional ways of life and must support themselves as plantation laborers. By themselves, peasants might simply erupt in spontaneous local revolts, but if the breakdown is widespread and if people can be organized into a nationwide movement, they become a force that can overthrow a government and take power. The aspiration for social justice itself is not enough. Another strong motivating force must be present: nationalism, the urge to overthrow colonial or foreign domination and achieve self-respect as a nation.

For people in the United States, part of the difficulty in understanding stems from confusion about the term itself. Some think of a "revolution" as being a simple barracks coup that involves no significant change in the lives of ordinary people. Others see it as an event full of meaningless violence. But for revolutionaries themselves, revolution means taking power in order to reorganize a society—and especially its economy—so that it serves the needs of the poor majority rather than those of a tiny privileged elite.

Many conservatives do not believe revolutions occur at all—at least not in the way we are defining them. They view revolutions as the work of small, externally influenced conspiratorial groups that take advantage of a government's weakness in order to seize power. Ultimately, revolutions are part of a larger totalitarian design. Such a mindset is not unlike that of segregationists in the South a generation ago. Attributing the civil rights movement not to injustice and black people's legitimate pressure for change, they saw it as a result of "outside agitators."

While most liberals concede that revolutions do occur (because of the shortsightedness and intransigence of elite groups), their response tends to be too little and too late, a vain hope that political tinkering, like "free elections," can prop up a tottering edifice.

If we wish to make sense out of U.S. policy in Central America, we must start by realizing that a revolutionary situation exists. In this and the following two chapters we will be seeking to understand how the United States has dealt with revolutions in Central America, how the debate has been framed in the United States, and most important, where the process is leading.

Turning to examine how events have unfolded since mid-1979, we shall identify some underlying patterns and trends. Readers should not be intimidated by the rush of names, dates, places, and acronyms. Instead they should concentrate on the overall thrust of the narrative, which indicates how steadily increasing U.S. involvement, far from addressing the Central America's real problems, has prolonged and intensified the conflicts, and has led to a U.S.-sponsored war in Central America.

REFORM VS. REVOLUTION

Revolutionary situations developed in Central America during the 1970s partly because U.S. administrations paid little attention to the region. They assumed, perhaps, that Central America was "secure"—so secure, in fact, that the CIA closed its station in El Salvador for a period in 1976 and 1977. In mid-1977 the Carter administration made El Salvador a partial "test case" for its human rights policy, delaying the appointment of a new ambassador for three months to express disapproval of government violence. However, when the ambassador arrived, saying he would make up his own mind about human rights abuses—despite the obvious evidence (see pp. 24–27), the Salvadoran military and oligarchy assumed that the U.S. human rights policy would have little bearing on their country.

In Nicaragua, Somoza's overthrow brought an abrupt change of tone in U.S. policy. Within days, Carter administration spokespersons were making programmatic statements, insisting that change was inevitable and that the key question was how to channel it. Reforms were necessary in El Salvador, Guatemala, and Honduras, they said—presumably in order to stave off revolution. William Bowdler, a senior diplomat, traveled through the region delivering this message to governments, armies, and business groups. For instance, he told Honduran army officers they should respect elections that lead to civilian government.

The Carter administration sought to deal with the Sandinista government, apparently hoping that U.S. aid could "moderate" it. Administration officials, however, seemed unclear about what "moderation" entailed and to what extent the Sandinistas could be influenced by U.S. aid. The administration advanced an immediate $10 million in emergency aid and put together a $75 million package of development aid, much of it destined for the private sector. Congress delayed the loan for several months, adding numerous conditions, some of which the Sandinistas considered to be violations of Nicaraguan sovereignty. It was an illusion to think that $75 million would offer the United States great leverage in Nicaragua—the Sandinistas obtained several hundred million dollars from international lending agencies and other governments, primarily European, during their first year and a half. It would be even more illusory to believe that a government like the Sandinistas would drop its revolutionary agenda and simply set up a parliamentary democracy like, say, Costa Rica's.

New revolutionary governments generally face hostility from other countries. Some ten countries made war on the USSR during its first few years, and more recently both Angola and Mozambique have had to contend with South African–backed guerrilla movements. Not only did the United States sponsor and organize the Bay of Pigs invasion against Cuba in 1961, but it invaded the Dominican Republic in 1965 to stop a mass movement that was attempting to restore the elected reform government of Juan Bosch, and contributed a great deal to the destabilization and overthrow of the democratically elected Allende government in Chile. With these and other examples in mind, the Sandinistas believed they would eventually be attacked by the United States, and began to plan accordingly. They invited Cuban advisors to help turn their guerrilla groups into an efficient army and police force, and to set up an efficient system for monitoring activities that might be "counterrevolutionary." That decision seemed logical, given Cuba's twenty years of withstanding attacks and covert actions from the United States. The United States would later speak of 2,000 or more Cuban "military advisors" in Nicaragua, but the number was more probably in the dozens at first, and then in the hundreds. Even in 1980, the Sandinistas were beginning to prepare a civilian militia.

Coup in El Salvador

A coup on October 15, 1979, shifted U.S. attention to El Salvador. For years a small but growing group of young officers, led by Captain (later Lieutenant Colonel) René Guerra y Guerra, had been meeting secretly to consider what to do about their country's problems. Planning for the coup took the better part of a year. In the crucial decision about who was to sit on the junta, the thirty-seven coup plotters at first voted for Colonels Adolfo Majano and Guerra y Guerra, both clearly reformers. However, by politicking among other officers, Colonel Jaime Abdul Gutiérrez, who was no reformer, replaced Guerra y Guerra. The consequences were serious. Guerra y Guerra and the other reformers would have liked to bring to justice President Romero, as well as many other individuals involved in torture and corruption. However, Gutiérrez and others prevented any significant changes. A few older officers were retired and others were shuffled around, but the institution remained unchanged. Colonel Gutiérrez managed to have his friend Colonel Guillermo García appointed defense minister. In terms of reform possibilities, the new government was stillborn.

The civilians on the junta and in cabinet posts were honest, competent, and sincerely desirous of reform—the cabinet of 1979 was perhaps the best in El Salvador's history. But their hopes and intentions were overwhelmed by events.

The left organizations concluded that the coup was an "imperialist" tactic and sought to challenge the new government. When the ERP guerrillas issued a call to insurrection and passed out weapons in two barrios of San Salvador, official troops came in and killed at least twenty-three people, most of them noncombatants. The popular organizations staged demonstrations, and unions occupied some factories. Military forces attacked the demonstrators and the workers, killing dozens. In November, the popular organizations halted their demonstrations, assuming that the new government's continued violence would reveal its true nature.

Although it viewed the new government as a hopeful sign, the Carter administration did little to aid the reform sectors, probably because it considered them too leftist. Already in August it had decided to renew military aid to El Salvador—even though there were far more human rights violations in 1979 than in 1977, when aid had been suspended. In November, the Pentagon sent a Defense Survey Team to assess the needs of the Salvadoran military.

The civilians in the Salvadoran government were not told of this visit. This was but one example of how little regard the military had for them. Another sign of the civilian officials' impotence was their inability to determine the fates of approximately 175 people who had "disappeared" under previous governments (any honest investigation would have pointed to military officers still in service). Most important, they could do nothing to stop the wanton attacks on the people. Although the Romero government had used repression to put down the rising militancy of the popular organizations, the numbers of those killed in 1977 and 1978 by government and right-wing groups could be still measured in the dozens. During 1979 the rate increased, and by October church human rights groups had documented over 300 deaths. Ostensibly this violence was one of the reasons for the October coup. Nevertheless, in December alone the number of people killed reached 281. The civilians in the government concluded that their presence was putting a reformist face on a bloodily repressive government and military. When they presented these issues to the military on December 27, Colonel Eugenio Vides Casanova told them, "We have put you into the position where you are, and for the things that are needed here, we don't need you. We have been running this country for fifty years, and we are quite prepared to keep on running it."

On January 3, 1980, the entire cabinet—except for Defense Minister García—resigned, as did most of the high-ranking civilian administrators. It was clear that those wielding the real power were hard-line military officers. In no way was El Salvador being governed by "moderates" caught between "extremists" of the right and left. Nevertheless, both the Carter and Reagan administrations repeated this characterization and made it a media stereotype for at least two more years.

At this critical juncture the Christian Democrats agreed to take over the government. Whatever their intentions, their main function was to lend plausibility to the "moderate" image. As a condition for entering the government, they demanded that some of the officers most involved in torture and murder be removed, and the army accepted. When it then reneged, however, the Christian Democrats did not withdraw as they had threatened. This pattern of impotence in the face of real power was to recur repeatedly.

Since their beginnings during the 1974–1977 period, the popular organizations had denounced each other's analyses and tactics. Even as late as 1979 they had not been able to march together in the same demonstrations. Now faced with a new level of repression, they stopped feuding long enough to form the Mass Revolutionary Coordinating Body. On January 22, 1980—the anniversary of the 1932 peasant uprising—some 200,000 people took part in a march, despite efforts by the military to prevent it and calls from Roberto D'Aubuisson for "patriots" to impede it (widely understood as a call to violence). This was probably the largest demonstration in Salvadoran history. As the march neared downtown San Salvador, snipers opened fire and at least twenty people were killed. The demonstrators rushed across town to the university, where they were surrounded by troops until the next day.

The level of everyday killing rose steadily. Ordinary citizens could be arrested, even shot, for breaking the curfew; yet death squads roamed at night, killing hundreds of people a month with impunity. During February, when a popular organization occupied the Christian Democrats' headquarters, troops attacked it over the protests of the party, killing four people, wounding others, and offering gross insults to the wives of prominent party leaders.

Ex-Major Roberto D'Aubuisson, who during his time in the National Guard and ANSESAL had gained a reputation for involvement in violence and torture, now appeared on television, naming people he considered to be "communists" (possibly from lists supplied by the CIA). Those named included Mario Zamora, the attorney general. When gunmen burst into Zamora's house and killed him, observers assumed that D'Aubuisson was responsible. Seeing these developments, those Christian Democrats with the most integrity, including junta member Héctor Dada, began to leave the government. José Napoleón Duarte replaced Dada on the junta.

Sensing the rapid deterioration, the United States pressed the military and the Christian Democratic government to enact a land reform program. On March 6, land reform and a state of siege were declared simultaneously. Troops moved out into the countryside, ostensibly to secure the 300 largest estates. However, these troops actually pursued, arrested, and killed peasants. Within days some 2,000 peasants had fled to San Salvador seeking protection—the first refugees of the war.

As initially announced, the land reform program was to have two phases: In phase I, the largest estates (above 1,250 acres) would become peasant-run cooperatives. Estate owners would be compensated by the government. Phase II of the plan (covering estates between 500 and 1,250 acres) would have affected the bulk of the nation's coffee production. It was never enacted. In May, a program designed to enable peasants to acquire the land they were sharecropping or renting was decreed. This additional program was the work of Roy Prosterman, a land reform expert who spoke no Spanish, but who had worked in Vietnam, designing a similar plan. The two programs even shared the same name, "Land-to-the-Tiller."

Since the coup, the archbishop of San Salvador, Oscar Romero, had been the most powerful moral voice in the country. He had angered some leftists by urging that the junta formula be given a chance, but he had also denounced the killing of civilians and defended the rights of the popular organizations. He had warned the United States not to send military aid, most notably in a letter to President Carter in February 1980. On March 23, as he ended his Sunday sermon, he reminded soldiers that the peasants were their brothers and sisters and that no human command is higher than God's law "Thou shalt not kill." Plainly, he was telling soldiers not to obey orders to kill civilians, and his words were heard on radio throughout the country. The next afternoon, a gunman stepped into the chapel where he was saying Mass and shot him. (Later there were persistent reports that Roberto D'Aubuisson and other military figures had had a hand in the murder.) Just as astonishingly, the archbishop's funeral was attacked with bombs and automatic weapons and at least twenty people were killed in the ensuing panic. For many Salvadorans the *lèse-majesté* shown here signified how far the forces of violence were prepared to go.

In April 1980, the popular organizations, political parties, labor unions, professional groups, and university and church groups formed the FDR (Revolutionary Democratic Front). The FDR was conceived as a political alternative to the Christian Democrat–military junta. Its program called for broad reforms that were similar to what the Sandinistas were attempting in Nicaragua. Enrique Álvarez, a dairy farmer and member of the oligarchy who had been minister of agriculture under the junta (and twice before), was named president.

Shortly before Romero's murder, Robert White had arrived as the new U.S. ambassador. He brought with him strong human rights credentials, particularly for the pressure he had exerted on the Stroessner dictatorship in Paraguay. In El Salvador, however, there was a crucial difference. It had been safe to pressure for human rights in Paraguay, since there was no viable alternative to Stroessner on the horizon. In El Salvador there existed a strong and organized left. To acknowledge the military's violence would undermine the legitimacy of the "reform" government and so favor the left.

Throughout 1980 El Salvador was sliding slow-motion toward insurrection. While one general strike in June was quite successful, another attempt in August was not. U.S. embassy spokesmen portrayed the August strike's failure as an indication of the diminishing appeal of the left. On May 14, a group of peasants fleeing an army "clean-up" operation were caught between Salvadoran and Honduran troops at the Sumpul River. Some 300 were slaughtered. Troops also attacked the National University in June, killing a number of students. The university was then closed; it was viewed as a center of opposition because it allowed the popular organizations to maintain offices there.

In May, some 1,197 noncombatants were killed by official troops or right-wing groups; for the rest of 1980 the average was over 700 a month. These killings were not primarily done in response to guerrilla violence, since it was only in July and August that guerrilla organizations began their offensive attacks. Rather, the killings were directed at the popular organizations. By this point, mere membership in a popular organization made anyone a target for the death squads. Sometimes those who were picked up, tortured, and killed were simply friends or relatives of organization members. As all possibility of nonviolent action seemed to be eliminated, many people began to participate directly in guerrilla organizations. Even people who were not involved in violence, such as those who were documenting human rights violations, lived in continual apprehension and fear. Some chose to leave the country.

With the example of Nicaragua still fresh in their memories, most Salvadorans waited expectantly for some sort of insurrection. Most observers believed that a prolonged guerrilla struggle could not occur in El Salvador because it was too small and too densely populated—there were few hiding places and no sympathetic countries on its borders. When it happened, the insurrection would be an all-out confrontation. (Events, of course, proved otherwise.)

Although the reform-minded officers had probably been outweighed by the hard-liners from the beginning, even before the coup, Colonel Majano's presence on the junta indicated that there was still a reform sector. Nevertheless, he was now shown to be impotent and even humiliated. When Roberto D'Aubuisson was caught red-handed in a coup attempt in May, Majano had him jailed. At that point the entire officer corps voted to have Colonel Gutiérrez replace Majano as head of the junta. D'Aubuisson was released.

In September 1980, Colonel García attempted to consolidate his own power by shifting reform-minded officers out of positions of power, especially troop command positions. Majano and others at first refused to accept the changes. Then, recognizing that they were outnumbered, and faithful to the military mystique of authority, they gave in. In December, Majano was finally thrown off the junta. The officers, recognizing the change in the wind after the election of Ronald Reagan, approved the move by a vote of 300 to 4. Majano immediately fled El Salvador. Within a few days José Napoleón Duarte was chosen to be president of the junta (not of the country).

As the leading Christian Democrat, a former two-term mayor of San Salvador, and as the candidate whom the military and government had kept from the presidency through electoral fraud in 1972, Duarte was undoubtedly popular. However, he had not been living in El Salvador during the crucial years of the 1970s, when the popular organizations had become central political actors, more militant and stronger than the political parties. To a great extent, events had passed him by. By the time he returned, the real agenda for El Salvador's elites, the military, and the United States was to prevent a Nicaragua-style revolution. The essential role would be played by the military. A Christian Democratic reform program could no longer solve the country's underlying problems and was useful only to the extent that it could provide some legitimacy for the forces seeking to prevent revolution. During Duarte's term as president of the junta (December 1980 to April 1982), some 15,000 noncombatants were killed by official and right-wing groups.

Guatemala: Struggle Intensifies

In Guatemala, events were reaching a comparable pitch. Since early 1979, guerrilla organizations—especially the EGP (Poor People's Guerrilla Army) and ORPA (People-in-Arms Organization)—had extended their influence in the countryside. Both organizations had substantial Indian membership.

Moreover, despite the systematic torture and murder of hundreds of people a year, labor unions, peasant organizations, and student and church groups were becoming more militant. In 1979, they had formed the Democratic Front Against Repression, which seemed to portend the eventual formation of a broad political front.

In January 1980, a group of Indian peasants from Quiché, together with some labor and student organizers, occupied the Spanish embassy, hoping to draw attention to the army's abduction and murder of dozens of their leaders. Police stormed the embassy—over the repeated protests of the ambassador—and a fire broke out, burning thirty-nine people alive, including embassy personnel. Spain suspended diplomatic relations. In Guatemala, the incident symbolized the obsessive ruthlessness of the power structure and was a sort of psychological watershed: many concluded that the country was headed toward the kind of insurrection that had already occurred in Nicaragua and seemed to be on the horizon in El Salvador.

About three weeks after the embassy occupation, plantation workers organized by CUC (Committee for Peasant Unity) went on strike in the cotton and sugar plantations on the southern coast. The strike spread as harvest workers commandeered vehicles to organize other plantations. Within a few days, the whole coastal plain, the country's main agroexport region, was at a standstill. It was the largest strike in Guatemalan history. Thousands of plantation workers gathered at one spot on the Pan-American Highway and kept vigil as troops with automatic weapons looked on. The government, its image still bloody from the Spanish embassy incident, agreed to raise the legal minimum wage in agriculture to $3.20 a day.

The level of violence and suffering in Guatemala certainly was quite comparable to that in El Salvador, and the Guatemalan army acted with fewer scruples. However, there was little direct U.S. involvement; and for the media, Guatemalan violence was so perennial that only the most bizarre incidents were reported.

Nicaragua: First Steps

In the meantime, the Sandinistas in Nicaragua were working methodically to consolidate their power and to give the revolution its basic direction. Starting with an empty treasury, they sought to carry out ordinary government functions, drawing on non-Sandinista administrators and even some former employees of the Somoza bureaucracy.

The new government held about a quarter of the prime farmland and some 120 major industries and businesses left behind by the dictator and his associates. These became the cornerstone of a new "mixed economy." Through its control of banking, finance, and foreign trade, as well as regulations on taxes and labor conditions, the government could set the parameters for a new economy.

Politically, the Sandinistas set out to involve as many people as possible through mass organizations: farm laborers in the Association of Rural Workers, urban workers in the Sandinista Central Labor Federation (which grew very rapidly alongside non-Sandinista unions that continued to function), neighborhoods in the Sandinista Defense Committees, as well as organizations for women, youth, professional people, and others.

The honeymoon between the Sandinistas and the anti-Somoza business and upper-class sectors lasted less than a year. The break came when the Sandinistas decided to change the formula for representation in the State Council to include more Sandinista grassroots representatives (alongside other representatives named by political parties, business and professional groups, and labor organizations). The Sandinistas argued that the rapidly growing mass organizations required greater representation. As a result, business and allied groups stood in a minority and could be outvoted. They were still overrepresented in comparison to the small percentage of the population they represented. Nevertheless, losing political power was a bitter pill for people accustomed to playing a dominant role (even though they had previously been overshadowed by Somoza).

Largely over this issue, Alfonso Robelo, a businessman who had been prominent in the later stages of the effort to overthrow the dictatorship, resigned from the junta, as did Violeta de Chamorro, the widow of *La Prensa* editor Pedro Joaquín Chamorro.

Dissension broke out at *La Prensa* itself as workers became increasingly unhappy with the paper's anti-Sandinista editorial line. When the board fired Xavier Chamorro after a dispute over editorial policy, he withdrew his stock (representing a quarter of the shares) and started *El Nuevo Diario*, a prorevolutionary paper. Three-quarters of the workers went with him. This split in the Chamorro family was not uncommon among the professional classes. Many remained committed to the Sandinista revolution because they judged it good for Nicaragua, even though it might involve surrendering some privileges.

Almost simultaneously with the rise of middle- and upper-class opposition to the Sandinistas, there appeared divisions in the Catholic church as well. Despite their misgivings, the Nicaraguan bishops had accepted the revolution. In November 1979, they had written a very positive pastoral letter encouraging Catholics to participate. Four priests occupied cabinet-level positions in the government, including Miguel D'Escoto, the foreign minister, and Ernesto Cardenal, an internationally known poet. However, less than a month after Robelo resigned, the bishops stated that the emergency period was over and that the four priests who occupied government posts should resign. (The priests in fact managed to stay at their posts for several years with some support from sectors in Rome, including Cardinal Casaroli, the Vatican secretary of state.)

In stressing the anti-Somoza credentials of Archbishop Obando and the other Nicaraguan bishops, commentators have failed to recognize that their positions throughout the 1970s had closely paralleled those of the opposition political parties and business groups like COSEP (High Council of Private Enterprise), the umbrella orga-

nization uniting business interests, in both tone and timing. The
bishops had opposed the Sandinistas; and they approved the insurrection only after almost all Nicaraguans, including the business sector, supported the revolution. It was really not surprising that they
would break with the Sandinistas just when the business and upper-
class sectors did so. However, this stance set the bishops at odds with
many Catholics, including priests and sisters, who saw the revolution in much more positive terms.

ENTER RONALD REAGAN

Although the reform efforts of the Carter administration were
largely ineffective, they had angered most right-wing Central Americans, who had a much more direct way of dealing with subversion:
kill as many "subversives" as necessary. These groups were greatly
encouraged by the tone of the 1980 Reagan campaign. One example
of that tone was provided by the Santa Fe Document, a blueprint
for a new Latin American policy drawn up by U.S. conservatives.
The document emphasized threats to U.S. security and proposed a
no-nonsense military approach to meeting those challenges. Only in
its last part did the paper even mention Latin American poverty, and
that only in a section proposing free trade as a cure-all for the region's economic ills. One of the paper's five authors, Roger Fontaine, received the Latin American post at the National Security
Council; and another, Louis Tambs, was later made ambassador to
Colombia. Even before his nomination, Reagan had sent envoys,
including Fontaine, to assure Guatemalan right-wing groups and the
military that they would be supported by a Reagan administration.
Wealthy Salvadorans celebrated Reagan's victory by firing their guns
into the air.

Insurgency in El Salvador

At this time there surfaced in Washington an anonymous document
called the Dissent Memo. Since dissenting voices are often edited
out as intelligence reports make their way from analysts up to policymakers, government agencies have set up dissent channels that
enable analysts to bypass normal channels if they feel their dissenting views are important. The Dissent Memo, dated November 6,

1980, appeared to be the work of disgruntled CIA, Pentagon, and State Department staff people who were alarmed over the direction of U.S. policy. It was an obvious appeal to the new administration to adopt a pragmatic approach in El Salvador—what it called a "Zimbabwe option." The idea was that the United States should seek a negotiated solution in El Salvador just as the conservative Thatcher government in Britain had promoted the internationally aided settlement in Rhodesia-Zimbabwe that led to the election of the Marxist, but independent, government of Robert Mugabe. The appeal went unheeded.

In fact, the election of Ronald Reagan may have encouraged a new boldness in political murder in El Salvador. On November 28, 1980, troops surrounded a Jesuit high school while members of the Maximiliano Hernández Martínez Brigade went in and dragged out six FDR leaders, including Enrique Álvarez. Their mutilated and tortured corpses were found the next day. Then, on December 2, three American sisters and one lay volunteer were abducted by National Guardsmen. At least two were raped; all four were killed. On January 4, gunmen, probably under the orders of military officers, strode into the coffee shop of the Sheraton Hotel in San Salvador and killed the Salvadoran head of the land reform program and two American labor advisors.

The United States suspended all aid after the killing of the churchwomen, but it reinstated economic aid after a few days and quickly doubled its military aid in the wake of the Salvadoran guerrillas' long-awaited "general offensive."

It was only in November 1980 that the five guerrilla groups had united to become the FMLN (Farabundo Martí National Liberation Front). The two largest groups were the Popular Liberation Forces, which was strongest in the area north of San Salvador, and the People's Revolutionary Army, which had its stronghold in the eastern part of the country. The other groups were the National Resistance (RN) (which had split from the ERP), the Salvadoran Communist Party, and the Revolutionary Party of Central American Workers (PRTC).

While many had been expecting an insurrection since early 1980, Ronald Reagan's election in November added urgency. Rebel leaders evidently hoped to present him with a *fait accompli* when he took office. They did not set in motion the broad Nicaragua-style insurrection they had hoped for—the murder of 10,000 civilians in 1980 had hit the popular organizations hard and had intimidated the population, especially in the urban areas. However, the offensive was in no way the "failure" the Salvadoran military and U.S. government prematurely declared it to be. In Santa Ana, the country's largest city, government troops revolted, killed the commander, destroyed the garrison, and joined the insurgency. The offensive was stopped without further U.S. aid, but the insurgents now held a significant part of the countryside.

President Reagan has correctly pointed out that his policies are a continuation of those begun by the Carter administration. Their reform rhetoric aside, by reinstating military aid to El Salvador and beginning large-scale military aid to Honduras, the Carter administration's policies had laid the groundwork for deepening U.S. military involvement. In September 1980, the United States forced El Salvador and Honduras to sidestep their disagreements remaining from the 1969 war; this truce paved the way for military cooperation. One of President Carter's final actions was to approve the sending of U.S. military advisors to El Salvador. During the offensive, Ambassador White announced that boats carrying arms from Nicaragua to FMLN guerrillas had been intercepted on a beach in eastern El Salvador. The report proved to be false—it was the first of many awkward attempts to blame the Sandinistas for the Salvadoran insurgency.

The Reagan administration's contribution to U.S. policy was to define the Central American conflict in a strictly East-West context. Indeed, as part of its effort to "hit the ground running," the new administration came into office eager to make Central America—especially El Salvador—a "test case" of American resolve. Apparently it felt that this offered an easy win, one that would send a message to Moscow and remove what it saw as the stigma of recent United States humiliations—the most ignominious being the Iranian hostage crisis. Central America seemed to offer a promising opportunity for "drawing the line"—and even beginning a "rollback."

Scarcely a month after the inauguration, the Reagan administration produced a white paper that claimed, on the basis of allegedly captured guerrilla documents, that arms were being shipped from Soviet-bloc countries through Cuba and Nicaragua to Salvadoran rebels. This white paper was subsequently shown to be based on unjustified extrapolations, false readings and translations, and quite possibly, forged documents.

The initial publicity barrage produced a backlash in the United States. The American public was skeptical that its security entailed support for armies that raped and killed nuns, and its fear that El Salvador might become a new Vietnam was expressed in both political cartoons and editorial pages. Government spokesmen suddenly lowered the volume of rhetoric, and Central America moved off the front pages.

Dealing with Nicaragua

With less fanfare the Reagan administration set about dealing with Nicaragua. The Republican platform had deplored the Sandinista revolution and promised to aid freedom-loving Nicaraguans. In February 1981, CIA director William Casey gave congressional intelligence committees a presidential "finding" that secret operations in Central America were important to U.S. national security.

The administration suspended both the $15 million still to be disbursed to Nicaragua from the Carter administration's $75 million package and credits for wheat purchases. Canada and other nations offered wheat, and the Soviet Union announced that it would supply a large amount—ironically, at the very moment the Reagan administration lifted the U.S. ban on wheat exports to the USSR. The Sandinistas meanwhile made the wheat issue a matter of nationalistic pride, organizing a "Corn Festival," which emphasized that corn was the authentic Nicaraguan grain.

In December 1981 President Reagan signed an order authorizing $19.5 million for anti-Sandinista exiles (called *contras*). According to the public record, these were the first monies to be funneled to them. However, since Somoza's fall, some several thousand former National Guardsmen had been camped in Honduras, and some had made sporadic raids across the border. It is reasonable to suspect that either the CIA or other U.S. agencies had been in contact with them, and that some money had already been channeled to their cause. Nicaraguan exiles had been receiving guerrilla training in camps in Florida and elsewhere. In April 1981, a group of exiles announced they would form a 600-man "freedom force."

The initial *contra* strategy was to occupy a portion of Nicaragua's sparsely populated eastern region and then declare it a "free territory." As *contra* attacks mounted, the Sandinistas decided to remove people from the areas along the Coco River and to militarize the zone. To do so, they forcibly relocated some 8,000 Miskito Indians farther inland in February 1982. This move alienated many Miskitos already offended by what they saw as Sandinista ignorance and insensitivity toward their culture and high-handed treatment. Moreover, at least one major Miskito leader, Steadman Faggoth, was already working with the *contras*, and he was able to lead many Miskitos to Honduran territory. There the CIA began training them as part of the *contra* forces.

In tandem with its military approach, the United States also used diplomacy. Assistant Secretary of State Thomas Enders visited Managua in August 1981, apparently to propose terms for a *modus vivendi* between the United States and Nicaragua: the United States would not support the *contras* or undermine the economy if Nicaragua did not support revolutions elsewhere. The Sandinistas could also read this proposal as a threat: it spelled out what the United States would do if Nicaragua did not satisfy U.S. conditions.

El Salvador: The 1982 Elections and Guerrilla Offensives

In late August, Mexico and France declared that the FMLN-FDR in El Salvador was a "representative political force" and that the conflict should be solved through negotiations. In effect, they were recognizing the insurgents as a legitimate political force. A number of Latin American countries—probably with U.S. prompting—labeled the declaration "intervention," but most nevertheless supported the principle of negotiation. Alarmed at these diplomatic developments and recognizing that the war in El Salvador was at a stalemate, a situation favoring the insurgents in the long run, the United States escalated its rhetoric in late 1981. Hinting at military action against Cuba, Secretary of State Haig threatened to go "to the source."

In January 1982, the Reagan administration produced its first congressionally mandated "certification" of progress in El Salvador on human rights, control of the armed forces, prosecution of those responsible for murdering Americans, land reform, and elections. The U.S. Congress had made such certification a condition for further aid. Human rights organizations unanimously rejected the administration's claims of improvement, but from that point onward the ritual of certification was repeated every six months.

Since mid-1981, the administration had urged its version of a "political" solution for El Salvador: elections in which the opposition could participate if it laid down its arms. Neither the army nor the death squads were expected to lay down *their* arms, however. In April 1981, Defense Minister García had appeared on television to present a public list of 138 "traitors," including all the prominent members of the opposition as well as people in the church and labor unions. From the FMLN's viewpoint, the October 1979 coup and the military-Christian Democratic government had been the power structure's response to the organized political movements of the poor. Elections by themselves could not solve El Salvador's problems, especially when the military was killing thousands of civilians a year.

The March 1982 election of members to the Constituent Assembly no doubt gave the Reagan administration's policies a welcome boost. The two major parties were the Christian Democrats, headed by Duarte, and the National Republican Alliance (ARENA), headed by D'Aubuisson. ARENA was related to the death squads: both grew out of the same soil, and they represented the political and military aspects of the oligarchy's overall strategy. ARENA also displayed some tactics borrowed from the United States: its colors were red, white, and blue, and it employed a Madison Avenue agency, McCann-Erickson, to write slick campaign slogans and design materials. At the village level, ARENA could use paramilitary force or threats.

Although the photogenic spectacle of thousands of Salvadorans lining up to vote in the hot sun was a boon to U.S. policy, the day after the election Ambassador Hinton faced a delicate problem. The Christian Democrats had won a plurality of votes, but ARENA and the other right-wing parties had won a majority in the assembly. D'Aubuisson himself was likely to become president instead of Duarte. Hinton made it quite clear that if D'Aubuisson were to be president, U.S. aid would be in jeopardy. Visitors from Washington such as Jim Wright, Democratic congressman from Texas, and General Vernon Walters, an ex-deputy director of the CIA with good hard-line credentials in Latin America, arrived to underscore the point. The military decided the president should be a neutral figure and chose Álvaro Magaña, making it clear to the Constituent Assembly, which duly elected him. Magaña had spent seventeen years as head of El Salvador's mortgage bank, where he had gained favor with military officers by granting them loans not justified by their income or credit rating. As president he had little real power.

ARENA had been deprived of the presidency, but it controlled the key economic cabinet posts, including the Ministry of Agriculture, and so it could block implementation of land reform programs and generally thwart any moves toward change. Behind ARENA, of course, stood the oligarchy itself.

Meanwhile the FMLN had steadily increased its military capabilities. In a series of major actions the guerrillas blew up a large bridge, the Puente de Oro, which was vital to the country's transportation, destroyed a good part of the Salvadoran air force in a January 1982 raid (probably with inside collaboration), and occupied a number of towns. In October 1982, the FMLN launched a major offensive and, at the same time, proposed "dialogue without preconditions" in a document that was hand delivered to the army and government by Archbishop Rivera. A chorus of right-wing voices denounced it, but some army field commanders wrote a letter saying that they, who were bearing the brunt of the fighting, thought it should not be rejected out of hand.

The Salvadoran armed forces did poorly in combat. The FMLN did not kill captives (as did the official forces) but released them to the International Red Cross. This policy reduced the official troops' motivation to fight and brought the FMLN good will as well as weapons.

The army's major success continued to be cowing the population by terror, such as the U.S.-trained Atlacatl Brigade's massacre of 482 people in Mozote in December 1981. Death-squad killing continued apace, and still no one was brought to justice for the murder of several Americans. Finally even Ambassador Hinton—who had expressly set out to placate the right wing, which had been alienated by Ambassador's White's reform efforts—felt obliged to make a statement. In an October 1983 speech to the American Chamber of Commerce in San Salvador, he said that a "mafia" was at work and had killed 30,000 people. Right-wing Salvadoran business people left in a huff. Hinton's position was undercut when the *New York Times* ran a first-page story in which an unnamed senior official (who later turned out to be William Clark, head of the National Security Council) expressed the administration's displeasure with the speech.

Guatemala: The 1982 Coup and Government Massacres

The Guatemalan army was meanwhile scoring success of a kind with little or no help from the United States. Having come to the conclusion that it faced an insurgency made up largely of Indians, it carried out a series of massacres in Indian villages in which most of the people were judged to be guerrilla collaborators or sympathizers. The media, however, focused more on the coup of March 1982, in which army officers overthrew General Romeo Lucas García. The moralizing tone of the new head of government, General Efraín Ríos Montt, the fact that he was a born-again Christian, and the temporary drop in killings by urban death squads (that is, plainclothes police) obscured the government's massacre policy in the mountains. The Reagan administration eagerly seized on Ríos Montt's image to claim an improvement in human rights. When the two met in December 1982, Reagan said he thought Ríos Montt had had a "bum rap." From Lucas García to Ríos Montt to General Mejía Victores, who replaced him, the Reagan administration repeatedly sought to send military aid to Guatemala, each time citing "improvements" in human rights observance.

It is impossible to calculate how many Guatemalans were killed in 1982. Estimates range from 3,000 to 10,000. Some 100,000 Indians fled to Mexico. The Guatemalan bishops claimed that one million people had been uprooted from their homes—a *seventh* of the population. In some cases the army relocated the Indians and in others it forbade them to travel outside their own villages. People caught in the open countryside could then by definition be regarded as guerrillas. Sometimes the army used counterinsurgency terminology familiar from Vietnam, such as "strategic hamlets" and "model villages." By forcing Indian males in each village to form a "civil patrol," they could at once administer a loyalty test (refusal would mark anyone as a subversive), force people to take sides, set in motion a vast patrolling system, and use the people as a buffer between themselves and the guerrillas. After each patrol session the Indians had to turn in their weapons, since the army did not trust them. The impact of such counterinsurgency techniques on the Indian way of life has been so serious that some have called it "ethnocide."

In the short run, the massacre strategy was successful. People were loathe to support the guerrillas, who had been unable to protect them from the army, and the guerrillas had to withdraw to more remote regions. The guerrillas lost their momentum, although their forces continued to pose a threat to the government.

The government's successes in Guatemala, with little U.S. aid, have undoubtedly strengthened the arguments of right-wing forces in El Salvador, who see as unfair and unrealistic the U.S. insistence on at least the appearance of reform together with its attempts to constrain the killing.

GETTING SET FOR THE LONG HAUL

The Reagan administration's anticipation of a quick win in Central America largely dissipated in 1981. An internal National Security Council memo of April 1982 indicated that the inner circle of the administration was beginning to take a long-range view of Central America. The memo recognized that a good part of the challenge would be to manage opposition to administration policy from European governments and Mexico, and dissent within the United States.

One source of frustration was the fact that the possibility of using proxy forces in Central America, especially those of Argentina, which had advisors in the region, disappeared after the United States sided with Britain in the Malvinas-Falklands War.

In the fall of 1982, a *Newsweek* cover story made the CIA's efforts in Nicaragua "covert" in name only. By this time what had started as a 500-man force now numbered 4,000. The United States was supplying the *contras*, funneling equipment through the Honduran army. The United States had also encouraged the promotion of General Gustavo Álvarez over his fellow officers to the position of defense minister; he was now the most powerful figure in Honduras. Many saw him and the U.S. ambassador, John Negroponte, as ruling the country in tandem, largely reducing Roberto Suazo Córdoba, the civilian president, to a figurehead. Guatemalan- and Salvadoran-style repression, including "disappearances," was well underway.

The *contras* themselves received a season of media attention. Reporters were especially fascinated by Edén Pastora. During the anti-Somoza struggle he had been in and out of the Sandinistas several times. In 1978 he had led the daring action of taking the whole National Palace hostage. It would seem that even then he had annoyed some of the other Sandinistas by becoming a media figure (called

"Commander Zero"), which was contrary to their practice of not seeking the limelight individually. After the downfall of Somoza, Pastora seems to have regarded his position as vice-minister of the interior as insufficient, given his popularity. The issue that he cited in explaining his withdrawal from the Sandinista revolution was Cuban influence. He left Nicaragua in 1981 and apparently became involved in some activity for the Guatemalan revolutionaries. However, he surfaced in April 1982 in Costa Rica and announced his intention to fight the Sandinistas, who promptly branded him a traitor.

What was most clear was that even as they grew in numbers and acquired heavier equipment, the *contras* remained based in Honduras and were unable to ignite any significant rebellion within Nicaragua. The reason would seem to be that the people regarded them as linked to the previous Somoza regime and to the CIA. An exception was the case of Miskito Indian *contras*, who for a time could capitalize on the Sandinistas' insensitivity toward their people and some instances of mistreatment.

In El Salvador, U.S. advisors were encountering problems in turning the Salvadoran armed forces into an efficient counterinsurgency force. U.S. advisors were upset with the Salvadorans' nine-to-five manner of fighting and their reliance on large troop movements instead of small guerrilla-style patrols for ambushing and moving at night. In January 1983 Major Sigifredo Ochoa, whom U.S. advisors respected (despite his political ties to D'Aubuisson) rebelled, refusing to accept a transfer order from Defense Minister García, who was seeking to shore up his own power base. Other officers supported Ochoa. The impasse was broken when Ochoa accepted a temporary post in Washington, on the condition that García resign. This move enabled U.S. advisors to speed up a purge of Salvadoran officers and replace them with those who agreed with U.S. tactics.

The results, however, were mixed. A "National Plan" modeled after "pacification" efforts in Vietnam was launched in mid-1983. The idea was that army units would sweep through areas in the provinces of Usulután and San Vicente and then remain to protect U.S.-funded civic action and development programs. The guerrillas dispersed with little fighting, and the development programs went ahead. Soon, however, it became clear that the FMLN, which still controlled the countryside, had decided to allow the programs to proceed since they provided jobs and services for the people. The result: U.S.-funded teachers were holding classes in guerrilla-controlled areas of El Salvador.

The Contadora Group

For some time, Latin American countries, especially Mexico and Venezuela, had worked to promote a diplomatic alternative to what they saw as a process headed toward regional conflagration. Mexico, Venezuela, Colombia, and Panama met in January 1983 on the Panamanian island of Contadora and launched a diplomatic effort. At first the Reagan administration ignored the "Contadora Group." Later it publicly professed support, while repeatedly undermining it. For example, in July 1983, just as the Contadora countries were producing their first comprehensive proposals, President Reagan dispatched navy fleets to the Pacific and Caribbean coasts of Nicaragua and announced that the largest U.S. military exercises to date, Big Pine II, would take place in Honduras during the fall. Similarly, in September, the Contadora countries, in consultation with the governments of Central America, drew up their Twenty-One Points, which provided guidelines for mutually agreed upon measures for either eliminating or reducing foreign military presence in the region. The document contained provisions on bases, military aid, and advisors, and measures to end the fomenting of revolution in other countries. Yet just as the Contadora countries were seeking to demilitarize the region's conflicts, the Reagan administration was attempting to revive CONDECA (the Central American Defense Council), a body for regional military cooperation, which had ceased to function after the downfall of Somoza. The United States hoped to unite the Salvadoran, Honduran, and Guatemalan armed forces in order to use them against the Sandinistas or the Salvadoran guerrillas. However, the plan failed when the Guatemalan army balked.

The Invasion of Grenada

Since entering office, the Reagan administration had indicated that it would not rule out military force if it were needed to protect U.S. interests. In September 1983 Fred Iklé, undersecretary of defense for policy, stated in a major speech, "Let me make this clear to you: We do not seek a military defeat for our friends. We do not seek a military stalemate. We seek victory for the forces of democracy."

An opportunity for U.S. military intervention in the region came in October, when internal feuding in Grenada's ruling New Jewel Movement and the murder of Prime Minister Maurice Bishop and his followers provided the opening for an American "liberation." In fact, during the "Ocean Venture 81" exercises on the Puerto Rican island of Vieques in 1981, U.S. forces had carried out a war game, the code name of which indicated that it was a rehearsal for an invasion of Grenada. The fictitious country had been called "Amber and the Amberines." (Grenada's formal name is "Grenada and the Grenadines," and there is a place near Port Salines called Amber; in the exercise "Amber" was supported by "Red," no doubt meaning Cuba.)

Many saw this as a kind of dress rehearsal for a U.S. attack on Nicaragua, in concert with its local allies, Honduras and El Salvador and perhaps Guatemala, who would allege Sandinista aggression, just as the neighboring tiny eastern Caribbean countries had provided the United States with a patina of legitimacy for the Grenada invasion. Nicaraguans began to dig air raid trenches and moved ever closer to a war economy. At the same time, Nicaragua took steps to remove any pretexts for a potential invasion by asking some Cubans and Central American revolutionaries to leave, announcing elections, and lifting some restrictions on the press. If these were concessions, the Reagan administration simply regarded them as proof that its pressure was working and as a signal for more.

The Kissinger Commission Report
and the 1984 Elections in El Salvador

The release of the Kissinger Commission report dominated the news about Central America in early 1984. Public debate focused largely on secondary issues: whether military aid to El Salvador should be conditioned on human rights improvements (as the report contended, with some dissenters, including Dr. Kissinger), and whether the United States should cut off aid to the *contras* (as two panel members believed). There was little public questioning of the overall framework of the report, which behind its apparent strong emphasis on development programs insisted that the United States must be able to "prevail" in Central America both for its national security and for its "credibility" worldwide. Nevertheless, neither Kissinger's prestige nor the carefully crafted appearance of bipartisanship reduced congressional or public opposition to the administration's policy.

During the first few months of 1984 there was another election drama in El Salvador, choreographed by the United States, even though some of the performers were unruly. Again, the lead roles were played by Duarte and D'Aubuisson. In the first election, held in March, none of the six participating parties received an absolute majority, thus necessitating a runoff. At that point, the United States was successful in preventing other right-wing parties from endorsing D'Aubuisson's ARENA party, and in preventing the ARENA-controlled assembly from making rule changes in its own favor. Duarte's narrow but sufficient margin—54 percent to 46 percent—was somewhat marred when it was revealed that the CIA had funneled $2.1 million into the campaign to aid Duarte, and that the Agency for International Development had used its influence to have a U.S.-supported peasant organization, the Salvadoran Communal Union, work for Duarte, giving him 300 campaign workers in the countryside.

The Reagan administration lost no time in bringing Duarte to Washington, where he melted congressional resistance. The administration was now able to obtain $70 million more in military aid and $135 million in economic aid for El Salvador.

THE U.S. MILITARY BUILDUP

Since 1979, policymakers had been acutely aware that the public was apprehensive about another Indochina-type war. At least in the short run, Reagan administration spokespersons had not overcome the "Vietnam syndrome" and found themselves repeatedly insisting that they had no intention of sending U.S. combat troops to Central America. Yet a *New York Times* story in April 1984 could begin: "The Pentagon is now in a position to assume a combat role in Central America should President Reagan give the order," and go on to survey the components of that readiness. Such preparation had occurred incrementally, with little fanfare and little scrutiny from Congress.

The United States had built up an impressive military infrastructure, especially in Honduras, often by using joint military maneuvers as the occasion to cut roads, extend airstrips, or erect buildings. The result was a network of semipermanent facilities. When Senator

James Sasser (D.-Tenn.) of the House Appropriations Committee drew attention to this buildup, Congress seemed more concerned about whether the Pentagon had overstepped any rules than about the combat intervention that the buildup portended.

The United States was engaged in an almost unending series of military maneuvers and maintained a continual military presence with phases of greater and lesser intensity. For example, the military exercises "Ocean Venture 84" and "Grenadier I" in spring 1984 together involved some 33,000 troops. Exercises in Honduras along the Salvadoran border were intended to intimidate Salvadoran guerrillas and disrupt their supply lines and escape routes. On similar exercises in 1983, U.S. armed forces were involved in various phases of the Honduran army's pursuit of guerrillas; and at that time, James Carney, an American priest who saw himself as their chaplain, was killed under mysterious circumstances.

However their participation in that operation might be characterized, U.S. armed forces personnel in El Salvador were deeply involved in the war, even if they were not combatants. In El Salvador the United States was directing the overall strategy of the war; U.S. reconnaissance flight data were being used to direct Salvadoran bombing; and U.S. pilots were sometimes accompanying Salvadoran fliers on combat missions. General Paul Gorman of the U.S. Southern Command reportedly recommended that the CIA attack rebel areas with unmarked AC-130 gunships, planes equipped with guns that can fire into every square foot of an area the size of a football field. In fact, the United States seemed to be moving more and more into an air-war strategy. The FMLN saw the increased use of helicopters and bombing as an attempt to drive the civilian population out of rebel-controlled areas.

The CIA was engaged in a myriad of activities with a reported 3,000 people on its payroll in Honduras. CIA personnel directed and engaged in sabotage raids from speedboats off the Nicaraguan coast, flew over Nicaragua to drop supplies and bomb targets, and directed the *contra* ground war. In some cases it was clear that those involved were non-Nicaraguan mercenaries.

Yet not all was clear sailing for the Reagan administration. On March 1, 1984, a Dutch ship hit a CIA-planted mine off Nicaragua and within days some twelve ships, including those of the USSR and of staunch U.S. allies like Great Britain, had been hit. When Nicaragua took the case to the International Court of Justice in the

Hague, the United States refused to accept the Court's jurisdiction for two years. There was a loud international outcry and both houses of Congress passed resolutions condemning the mining, prompting the administration to suspend this particular tactic.

In the meantime, the CIA had been seeking to convince the *contra* forces to unite, but Edén Pastora refused to join with the FDN because its leaders were Somocistas. Pastora's prime asset had been his anti-Somoza credentials, but he was apparently considered too unreliable and erratic. The divisions were revealed most clearly when a bomb went off at a Pastora press conference, killing a journalist and wounding Pastora himself. Alfonso Robelo, who headed ARDE, Pastora's political organization, linked up with the FDN but apparently took few troops with him. The Sandinistas took advantage of the disarray to unleash a very successful offensive near the Costa Rican border, largely disbanding the Pastora/ARDE forces.

In Honduras, General Gustavo Álvarez, who had seemed to be ruling the country in tandem with John Negroponte, the U.S. ambassador, was suddenly overthrown by a coup in April 1984. Although Honduras continued to be ruled by the army, a group of some thirty officers were now making the important decisions collectively. Part of their motivation was chagrin at the extent to which the United States had penetrated their country. They said they had become "prostitutes" and, at the very least, they were determined to demand a higher price for the services their country was rendering. The Honduran officers were incensed that the United States was training more Salvadoran soldiers than Hondurans in the regional military center it had set up on their territory, and they recalled how El Salvador had attacked their country and humiliated them in the 1969 war. At some future point, the same army might attack them again. Conceivably, they were also considering the probable results if U.S. policy were carried to its logical conclusion—a region-wide war in which all parties, Honduras included, would lose. On the other hand, if the United States ceased supporting the *contras*, Honduras might have to deal with 10,000 heavily armed unemployed killers.

Similarly, there was a continuing tug of war among the Costa Rican elites. Some believed that the Sandinista threat was such that Costa Rica should be diplomatically allied with the United States in its attempt to isolate Nicaragua, and should allow the *contra* groups to use Costa Rican territory. Others feared that Costa Rican neutrality and democracy, the very identity of the country, would be undermined by such a course. Moreover, they insisted that Costa Rica's energies should go into dealing with its own economic crisis. In mid-1984, when Costa Rica accused Nicaragua of shooting into its territory (presumably at fleeing *contras*), the United States wanted to exacerbate the tensions; but with the aid of the Contadora countries, the two countries managed to lower the tensions.

The Guatemalan army and government continued to resist U.S. efforts to unite the armies of the region. This reflected no predisposition for peace (internally Guatemala's repressive policies had created a "nation of prisoners," according to the human rights organization Americas Watch) but simply a judgment that their interests did not require being subordinated to regional U.S. strategy.

During middle to late 1984, the Reagan administration was ready —even poised—for further intervention. Yet it sought to avoid any major new commitments that might alarm the public during the U.S. electoral campaign.

In September the Contadora Group circulated draft treaties to the Central American countries for their comments. The Sandinista government announced that it was accepting them with no modification. The Reagan administration was caught off guard and made its displeasure evident. It then conferred with its allies, Costa Rica, El Salvador, and Honduras, which raised a number of objections. The whole Contadora process seemed to be put back in limbo.

In early October, President Duarte gave a speech at the United Nations General Assembly in which he proposed to meet directly with the FMLN-FDR in the Salvadoran town of La Palma. The press saw this as a bold gesture for peace. However, the FMLN-FDR had already made repeated proposals for talks to be held in El Salvador. The desire of many Salvadorans for peace was evident from the number of white flags people carried in the crowds. With Archbishop Arturo Rivera y Damas as moderator, Duarte, other government officials, and top military officers met with FMLN commanders and FDR political figures in a respectful five-hour session. They agreed to meet for further discussions, but their positions remained far apart. For Duarte and the military (and the United States), the only thing to be negotiated was opposition participation in elections. For the opposition, however, such elections would solve nothing; what was required was a broad coalition government that would eliminate the killing of civilians and begin to deal with the country's underlying problems, as well as initiate a valid political process.

Ronald Reagan's re-election victory seemed to portend a deepening U.S. involvement—and quite possibly in direct combat. Whether the administration believed it had a mandate to act soon, or preferred to wait for the most opportune moment, whether escalation would happen rapidly, or by slow increments, remained to be seen.

THREE

CONFRONTING REVOLUTION: PATTERNS AND ISSUES

What is the United States up to in Central America?

"Stopping revolution" would seem to be a coherent and comprehensible answer.

The public debate would be better served if policymakers would indeed state their aims in such straightforward language. Then it could focus on whether such an aim is desirable or even attainable; and, if so, it could assess both the price and whether the American people are willing to pay it.

However, the terms of the debate often obscure matters. At first glance, the Kissinger Commission report would indicate that United States aims are economic development and the promotion of democracy. The military component of U.S. policy is primarily a means— a "shield"—toward those ends. President Reagan has told the public that the United States is giving three times more economic than military aid to the region. Others have focused on human rights or popular elections as though these issues in themselves were, or should be, the central element.

This and the following chapter will examine the overall trends of U.S. policy toward Central America, which was just surveyed in Chapter 2. The present chapter takes up themes common in public debates in the United States, while Chapter 4 seeks to understand where the policy is heading. In the overall flow of events, a number of patterns or tendencies are clearly discernible.

PATTERNS IN U.S. POLICIES

Despite the appearance of sharp liberal-conservative differences over Central America, U.S. policies show considerable continuity. The military track goes back to mid-1979, when the Carter administration made a basic decision to renew military aid to El Salvador, even before the "reform" coup. Prior to that, of course, there was a counterinsurgency side to the Alliance for Progress in the 1960s, and long before that, a history of direct U.S. intervention in the region that Latin Americans have not forgotten. The groundwork for the continuing expansion of the military approach was laid prior to the inauguration of Ronald Reagan. Conversely, the Reagan administration has been obliged to retain those elements of the Carter policy such as land reform that provide some legitimacy to U.S. policy. One ironic result was that in 1984 the CIA found itself putting money into José Napoleón Duarte's campaign in order to defeat Roberto D'Aubuisson, long a CIA "asset."

United States involvement in Central America has steadily deepened. In 1978 economic aid to the region was $86.9 million and military aid a mere $4.1 million (with none to El Salvador). In 1980 military aid totaled $59 million, while economic aid had reached $228 million. By 1984 military aid had reached a staggering $600 million, while economic aid stood at $196 million. This growth was most startling in El Salvador, where by 1983 military aid had reached $281.8 million and economic aid $87.1 million. These figures are all the more astonishing considering that the total budget for the Salvadoran government had been put at around $800 million. Moreover, these figures do not include what had come out of the Pentagon budget (maneuvers and military installations), CIA funds, nor disproportionate amounts of aid from international lending agencies arranged through pressure from the United States.

Since the United States is paying the bills, it is not surprising that it has come to take a preponderant role throughout the region both militarily and politically. In El Salvador, U.S military advisors began by supplying new equipment and technical instruction, but before long were not only designing overall strategy but overseeing its implementation in the field. To find the right leadership to implement such strategy, they pressured for major purges in the officer corps. By early 1984, U.S. personnel were directing the Salvadoran air force on which targets to bomb. The electoral processes in El Salvador in 1982 and 1984 largely served to legitimize the Salvadoran government in the eyes of the U.S. public and Congress. To achieve that end, the administration was not above heavy-handed tactics, such as Ambassador Hinton's intervention to prevent the assembly from making Roberto D'Aubuisson president in 1982 and CIA funding for the Duarte campaign in 1984.

The CIA's anti-Sandinista effort grew from the sponsorship of a 500-man sabotage group to the maintenance of a 10,000-man army. U.S. policy in Costa Rica and Honduras put U.S. geostrategic concerns above those countries' own development problems. With the collaboration of General Álvarez in Honduras, the United States built or upgraded about eight airfields, several new bases, and a training center. Honduras was thus turned into a platform for future U.S. military intervention. In September 1983, a Pentagon spokesman hinted that in order to resist Marxist expansion, the United States might have to establish a military presence in Central America similar to the one it maintains in Korea. Shortly afterwards, a delegation representing the Honduran business elite proposed to the Kissinger Commission that Honduras establish a Korea-type relationship with the United States.

Those who articulated U.S. policy became increasingly ideological and hard-line in their outlook. The Reagan administration replaced a number of diplomats experienced in Latin American affairs with people who had strong anticommunist credentials but no knowledge of the area. Subsequently, even some of those were replaced. Assistant Secretary of State Thomas Enders, a hard-liner who had helped direct the bombing of Cambodia and conceal it from the press and Congress, was nevertheless deemed too accommodating when he advocated a negotiated approach in Central America. He was replaced in mid-1983. By 1984, many believed that General Paul Gorman, the head of the U.S. Southern Command in Panama, had more influence on U.S. policy than ambassadors in the region.

Domestic opposition to the thrust of U.S. policy has been a great restraining factor. Many people, fearful of another Vietnam, clearly saw the dangers in Central America very early. The rape and murder of the American churchwomen, as well as other Americans, and the patent inability of the U.S. government to have those responsible brought to justice despite the Salvadoran military's dependence on the United States, had augmented the sense of outrage. Opinion polls consistently showed that more than 60 percent of the public disapproved of the administration's policy toward Central America.

Such figures could be misleading. For most people, Central America remained a remote region that had no direct bearing on their everyday lives. However, for a small but continually growing number of Americans, Central America has become a vital concern. Many have had firsthand experience as missionaries or development workers. Most churches in Central America, both Catholic and Protestant, have opposed the military thrust of U.S. policy and advocated negotiated approaches. Churches in the United States have acted as their sounding board. At the local level, both clergy and laity have played an important role in publicizing the effects of U.S. policy. Through the Sanctuary Movement, in which local congregations illegally offered public sanctuary to Salvadoran or Guatemalan refugees, they have dramatized the U.S. government's refusal to acknowledge the legitimacy of refugees' claims that their lives were endangered in their own countries.

By the mid-1980s, there were over twenty national organizations and over a thousand local groups around the country involved in public education on Central America, all constituting an embryonic antiwar movement.

Faced with a skeptical public, the Reagan administration devoted considerable attention to "selling" its policy. Both the State Department and the White House set up offices to present the administration view. For example, the White House Outreach Working Group on Central America staged frequent briefings in Washington, and the administration organized speaking tours for anti-Sandinista Nicaraguans around the United States and Europe. Initially President Reagan had kept some distance from Central America policy, but now he was forced to place his own personal prestige behind it. In April 1983 he addressed both houses of Congress, something that presidents had done only a few times in history. In May 1984 he made a prime-time address on national television.

The rationale for U.S. policy became increasingly simple, as the Reagan administration slowly abandoned the reform framework it had inherited. Its language sought to portray a sharp contrast between villains (the Sandinistas, who had "betrayed" their revolution, and the Salvadoran guerrillas, who would "shoot their way" into power) and heroes (the *contras*, who were called "freedom fighters," and the "democratic" Salvadoran government).

Democratic party opposition to the thrust of Reagan Central American policies has been primarily reactive, episodic, and piecemeal; it has been tied to particular pieces of legislation or particular events such as the Congressional outcry when the CIA mining of Nicaraguan harbors damaged European ships. Responding to constituent pressure, Democrats attempted to slow the more reckless developments by tying military aid to El Salvador to human rights "certification," and by chipping away at funding levels. Without such restraining actions, the present administration's policy would have moved even faster toward direct intervention.

Perhaps more than they would prefer to admit, many Democrats and liberals share the Reagan administration's premises. The differences are often over means and emphasis. Liberals tend to believe that problems in Central America can be solved by fine-tuning the mix of military and economic aid. Some may advocate negotiation, but they dare not spell out clearly where this might lead. During their television debates, both Walter Mondale and Geraldine Ferraro failed to challenge President Reagan and Vice-President Bush when they made statements that wildly distorted reality in Central America.

DEBATE THEMES

The major issues in U.S. policy debates over Central America concern violence, arms flows, and land reform. The focus of most discussions in the United States, however, is often far from the experience of Central Americans. The media concentrate on events with a direct U.S. connection while ignoring more crucial ones. For instance, hundreds of journalists descended on El Salvador to cover the U.S.-sponsored elections, but there was next to no coverage of the ARENA party's actions in the Salvadoran assembly to nullify the land reform program, and very little on the impact of bombing and strafing on civilians. The administration's semiannual certification of human rights progress caused some polemics about body counts in El Salvador, but the systematic massacre of thousands of Guatemalan Indians went unnoticed. Consistently, the media tend to judge the significance of events from the vantage point of Washington.

Thus the efforts of the Contadora countries were given only per-functory coverage, and one would be hard pressed to find any de-tailed discussion of their proposals or of their rationales in diplo-macy, until September 1984, when the Reagan administration was chagrined by Nicaragua's acceptance of the Contadora draft treaties.

Let us now look at some of the major debate issues and how they are framed.

Nicaragua

The standard U.S. view of Nicaragua might be stated as follows: After making an alliance with middle-class moderates to overthrow Somoza, the Sandinistas have "betrayed" the original revolution. They have restricted press freedom, limited the private sector, and attacked churches; their policies toward the Miskito Indians have been cruel and even genocidal; they have become proxies of Cuba and the Soviet Union, and their military buildup and export of rev-olution represent a clear threat to neighboring countries.

The intensity of these characterizations may vary but the general thrust is similar. The only positive statement the Kissinger Commis-sion could make about Nicaragua was that its government "has made significant gains against illiteracy and disease." Its criticism is oth-erwise obsessive and unceasing (pp. 4, 25–27, 30–31, 32, 33, 84–91, 93, 100, 113–116, 118–119, 126–127). Administration repre-sentatives such as Jeane Kirkpatrick and President Reagan himself recite litanies of Sandinista offenses. For their part, few Democrats dare to venture a good word about Nicaragua.

Before we accept the standard characterization, we might ask some questions. Who is to judge whether the Sandinistas have be-trayed the revolution? the Nicaraguan elites? Henry Kissinger? President Reagan? What would a cross-section of Nicaraguans—giving full weight to the poor majority—think of the way their gov-ernment is described by the Kissinger Commission report or by the U.S. press?

The evidence so far shows that most Nicaraguans accept the San-dinista government and many are enthusiastic supporters. A former prominent U.S. diplomat in Managua estimated that 80 percent of the people would risk their lives to defend the revolution. The ve-hement opponents for the most part come from the elites whose privileged lifestyles are threatened as the revolution takes its course.

Moreover, most governments in the world do not share the U.S. view of Nicaragua. Western European countries have sent several hundred million dollars in development aid, and Latin American countries maintain normal diplomatic and trade ties with Nicaragua.

The point here is not whether the Nicaraguan revolution is good or bad in itself. Rather, it is that the Sandinista government enjoys a basic legitimacy from its own people and from the international community. Whether poor Nicaraguans *should* welcome the *contras* as "freedom fighters" or not is irrelevant to U.S. foreign policy: the fact is that they do not.

The aim here is not to take up the conventional view of Nicaragua and refute it point by point. Rather, it is to suggest a way of looking at Nicaragua that will provide a more solid basis for U.S. policy.

As noted in Chapter 1, the Somoza dictatorship was overthrown by a revolutionary movement. It was neither the Sandinistas nor the upper- and middle-class moderates who overthrew Somoza—it was the ordinary Nicaraguans who took such steps as setting up barricades, taking over the towns, and providing help to the FSLN combatants. Almost all of the 40,000 who died came from among the poor. Few members of the anti-Somoza elite died unless they joined the Sandinistas.

Those who risked their lives did so not simply to overthrow a dictatorship and then to hand power over to the country's business elites. They were struggling to make basic changes in their country. That is what the Sandinista government has set out to do. The dramatic improvements in health care and education are for them a central feature of what revolution should mean.

Most Nicaraguans accept the idea that such a revolution requires a strong political force, a revolutionary party. Before automatically assuming that a two- or multiparty system is best, we should recognize that in Latin America real political power has traditionally been held by small elites of oligarchies and armies, even where formal democracy seems to function, as in Costa Rica or Venezuela. Elections may be honest and political parties may enter and leave office in an orderly fashion, but elites still hold the decisive power. In Nicaragua, many people believe that their revolutionary organizations, unions, and block committees give them a role in politics that is ongoing and is not merely activated for elections. They view the revolution itself as a form of democracy.

The basic division in Nicaragua is along class lines, between those who see the revolution as offering hope for their future and those who see it as diminishing their power and prestige. Naturally, opponents of the revolution do not refer to their own interests but to such principles as political pluralism, free enterprise, freedom of the press, and freedom of religion.

As noted in Chapter 2, the Catholic church itself is split over the revolution. The bishops' anti-Sandinista stand has its roots in their close association with anti-Somoza business and upper-class groups during the 1970s. The honeymoon ended for them at the same time it did for the business opposition. Alfonso Robelo resigned from the junta in April 1980, and in May the bishops told the priests in government posts they should leave (see p. 43). Many ordinary Nicaraguan Catholics are scandalized that their bishops, who have frequently criticized the Sandinistas, have never raised their voice to protest the CIA-directed *contras*, who by mid-1984 had inflicted 7,000 casualties, most of them civilians.

Similarly, *La Prensa*, which the U.S. media describe as an "independent" newspaper, is viewed quite differently by ordinary Nicaraguans. To begin with, for about half the population, it would be unthinkable to buy *La Prensa* since it would take 5 percent or more of a day's income. In any case, most see *La Prensa* as a weapon being used against the revolution. (The CIA worked with the Chilean newspaper *El Mercurio* in its efforts to overthrow the elected Allende government.) *La Prensa* is not "independent" of the elites. Some Nicaraguans would no doubt prefer to see *La Prensa* closed, and that is no doubt a temptation to the Sandinistas, who have thus far sought to maintain some measure of press freedom even when under military attack. The point here is modest enough: the whole question of *La Prensa* looks quite different when viewed from the angle of most Nicaraguans.

Again, after forty-five years of complete subservience to the United States under the Somozas, most Nicaraguans are proud of their new independence. As citizens of a nonaligned country and as members of the international community, they feel free to maintain a warm relationship with Cuba and to welcome collaboration from other socialist countries. By one count there were 1,200 technical assistants from socialist countries in Nicaragua, alongside 3,400 from Europe and the Americas. Some Cubans have worked with the Nicaraguan army and police, but there is no public proof for the administration's assertions that 2,000 or more Cubans are in Nicaragua for that purpose. Having lost 2.5 percent of their population in the war against Somoza, Nicaraguans feel a special bond with the struggles of people in El Salvador and Guatemala.

Many Americans who have gone to Nicaragua conclude not only that the negative stereotyping is wrong, but that, indeed, the Sandinista revolution is an exciting social experiment, a fresh approach to solving the problems of underdevelopment. Many people throughout Latin America see in Nicaragua a sign of hope.

However, one need not be a believer in the Nicaraguan revolution to recognize that the Sandinista revolution enjoys a great deal of support, especially from the bulk of ordinary Nicaraguans. U.S. government representatives and reporters, who almost always gravitate to elites, will tend to attribute to those elites a disproportionate importance. That was clearly the case with the Kissinger Commission, which talked with Sandinista government officials, with representatives of the business and upper-class opposition, and with the *contras*, but had no meaningful contact with ordinary Nicaraguans.

Yet it is precisely the experience and viewpoint of those ordinary Nicaraguans that must form the basis of an adequate policy toward the Nicaraguan revolution.

The Arms Flow to El Salvador

Since early 1981, the Reagan administration has insisted that the Salvadoran insurgents have been receiving substantial arms and ammunition shipments from Nicaragua (and therefore from Cuba, and ultimately the Soviet Union). In fact, this putative arms flow has become the Reagan administration's definition of the problem. All other considerations such as the history of the region, the atrocities by armies and police, and world public opinion are shoved aside as irrelevant.

What must be emphasized is quite simple: *at no point has the Reagan administration furnished convincing public proof for its repeated assertions that Nicaragua has sent massive and continual arms shipments to the Salvadoran rebels.*

The United States has spent tens of millions of dollars for communications and monitoring equipment in Honduras and in the Gulf of Fonseca. Honduran, Salvadoran, and U.S. soldiers, as well as *contras*, are continually patrolling the zones of alleged shipping. In spite of all this, no significant arms shipment has ever been intercepted.

Efforts to provide proof have repeatedly turned out to be embarrassing, such as the 1981 white paper or the 1982 case of Orlando Tardencillas. This young Nicaraguan was flown to a Washington press conference to testify that he had been sent to El Salvador by the Sandinistas. Instead, he denied it, saying he had been tortured by the Salvadoran military.

Reporters and film crews in rebel-held territory have found a heterogeneous assortment of weapons rather than the uniform equipment one would expect if there were systematic shipments. Most observers agree that the insurgents get much of their weapons from the Salvadoran army—from soldiers who surrender or from corrupt officers willing to sell them.

Nevertheless, there are indications that some substantial arms shipments were made at the time of the FMLN's January 1981 general offensive. Remarks later made by Fidel Castro to a West German politician seem to indicate Cuban involvement. The weight of the evidence, however, suggests that there have been no large-scale arms shipments since early 1981, although radios and medicines may have been sent.

Assuming that there was some Sandinista involvement in arms shipments in late 1980 and early 1981 and that it ceased partly because of the get-tough stance of the new Reagan administration (and perhaps because of a reassessment of the FMLN's prospects), we may appreciate a fine irony: the Reagan administration cannot take credit for its success in stopping the arms flow, for it needs just such an arms flow to justify its hostility toward Nicaragua and to explain the Salvadoran insurgency.

Death Squads and Massacres in El Salvador

Much of the debate on Central America has swirled around human rights, especially the question of death squads. People are disturbed that the United States is propping up a government in El Salvador that cannot find and prosecute those who murder Americans and is involved in the murder of tens of thousands of its own citizens. In response, defenders of the policy have offered a series of justifications: that both right and left kill and it is impossible to determine who is responsible, that human rights groups are biased, that the Salvadoran system of justice is ineffectual, or that violence is part of

Salvadoran culture and can be eradicated only over the long haul and only after a return to democracy.

Our interest here is not primarily to add to the polemics but rather to ask whether there is any coherent explanation for this violence. Is it "rational" from any point of view? Or is it entirely irrational and counterproductive, and serving the interests of the left, as some have asserted?

To answer, let us recall that during the 1970s there developed broad peasant-based opposition movements in El Salvador. They encountered violence from official forces and from ORDEN, the army's paramilitary organization; but until the beginning of 1979, the rate of killings and disappearances was not more than a few dozen a year. By October 1979, however, over 300 people had been killed. In December alone—during the first few weeks of the "reform" junta—the Catholic church documented 281 civilians killed by official or right-wing paramilitary groups. In 1980 over 10,000 were killed.

This violence was aimed not at guerrilla groups, which began their insurrection attempt only in January 1981, but at the popular organizations. It was effective in that public nonviolent opposition became impossible after mid-1980.

By mid-1984, the Catholic church estimated that 50,000 people—1 percent of the population—had been killed, the vast majority being noncombatants killed by official forces or right-wing paramilitary groups.

According to the conventional stereotype, the Salvadoran government is battling 6,000 to 10,000 guerrillas who have little popular support. If that is the case, what explains the large number of civilian deaths? It is more reasonable to view the opposition as a pyramid, with the guerrillas at the top, followed by a layer of "militia" (village people with some military training whose function is defensive), and then a much larger group of people who support the opposition cause, many of whom have been members of the popular organizations. They may give food to the FMLN, run messages, warn of the army's movements, or serve in other ways. Some may simply be sympathizers. They may be teachers or union leaders, doctors or village catechists.

From the viewpoint of the military and the power structure in general, all these people—the whole pyramid—are the enemy and all may be killed legitimately. For example, when stepped-up aerial bombing led to more civilian deaths, Salvadoran officers shrugged it off, saying that the casualties were *masas* ("masses"—that is, people supportive of the FMLN), in effect eliminating the distinction between combatants and civilians.

Certainly some of the killing is the work of actual death-squad groups who believe they are patriots fighting a so-called dirty war. The main leaders are military, but many of the participants are civilians.

For a long time the Reagan administration played down the death squads. However, in the fall of 1983, it began a highly visible campaign to bring them under control, culminating in the visit to El Salvador of Vice-President Bush, who reportedly brought with him a list of officers who should be transferred or disciplined. Duarte made death squads a major campaign theme and promised to move against them.

However, it is misleading to focus on the death squads as though these irregulars were the only forces at work. Official troops in uniform have been responsible for the largest number of civilian murders, sometimes in large massacres as at the Sumpul River in 1980 (300 victims), at Mozote in 1981 (382 victims), at Copapayo in 1983 (123 victims), and dozens of smaller incidents. The Mozote and Copapayo massacres were carried out by U.S.-trained troops.

What must be grasped is that such killings are not "aberrations," "excesses," or "abuses," but rather de facto policy. Moreover, they have been successful in stopping the popular organizations, breaking up their networks, and preventing further mass nonviolent resistance. This violence enables the military to hold onto the urban areas of the country. Without it, there would no doubt be crippling general strikes and other forms of massive nonviolent resistance.

Hence, it is chimerical to think that placing conditions on military aid or shuffling a few officers can ultimately halt what has been an essential element of a governmental policy of counterinsurgency.

Land Reform in El Salvador

The major characteristics of the land reform program in El Salvador were discussed in Chapter 2; there we pointed out that it was designed and imposed by the United States, and that it did not affect most of the coffee-producing lands. The Land-to-the-Tiller program has been marked by violence. One peasant leader estimated that

2,600 people had been murdered merely for applying for land. In 1983, peasant leaders said that 9,067 peasants had been evicted (out of 50,966 families who had applied for land). While many received "provisional" titles, only a token number received definitive land titles.

Behind the statistics is a simple fact: At the local level, landowners still have decisive power. Indeed, many military officers are themselves medium-sized landowners. The land reform program threatens their own interests. Landowners clearly resent the United States' imposition of land reform and are convinced that defeating the insurgency is a straightforward matter of killing "subversives" and has nothing to do with reforms. They have shown their ability to stymie U.S. proposals. Some have claimed that as many as 24 to 29 percent of El Salvador's landless peasants have benefitted from the land reform program, but on closer examination no more than 10 percent of the landless have actually done so.

The U.S. media and Congress have tended to ignore how much the oligarchy has thwarted the land reform program. From the beginning, the proposed Phase II (originally intended to apply to properties of between 500 and 1,250 acres, the heart of the coffee-producing land) was stopped. In his 1984 campaign, José Napoleón Duarte assured the coffee growers' association he would not apply Phase II unless the assembly voted for it (an unlikely event given the predominance of right-wing parties). Less than a month after Duarte's inauguration, the assembly suspended the Land-to-the-Tiller program. The vice-minister of agriculture admitted that "the land reform program is now formally paralyzed." Previously this program had been extended because of pressure from the United States. On this occasion, Duarte expressly asked the U.S. Congress not to make land reform a condition for sending further military aid.

Not only has the land reform program not worked—it cannot work under the existing regime. To work it would have to give land to a significant portion of the landless rural population. That would require the expropriation of a much larger area from the oligarchy, something the government will not do. In its present shape, the land reform program is largely a public relations effort to legitimize the Duarte regime in the United States.

The land reform program illustrates an ongoing contradiction in U.S. policy. U.S. policymakers believe some reform is necessary in order to undercut the appeal of the left, but they are unwilling to acknowledge the oligarchy's effective veto power over the Salvadoran government. The present land reform program contains enough conditions to alienate the landholding class, but not enough to produce basic structural change, just as occasional U.S. concern about human rights is enough to anger right-wing officers and death-squad leaders, without fundamentally affecting their ability to murder with impunity.

Elections and Democracy

The 1982 and 1984 elections in El Salvador were undeniably successful for the Reagan administration in that they undercut criticism of its policy. Similarly, the policy defenders can point to elections in Guatemala and Honduras and the stable democracy of Costa Rica in contrast to Nicaragua's Sandinista rule and a "sham" election in 1984.

At first glance, elections may appear to be the very essence of democracy, as long as there is freedom of the press and of assembly and votes are counted honestly.

However, there are other factors involved. It is interesting to note that etymologically the word "democracy" makes no reference to elections but simply to the "people" (Greek *demos*) and "rule" or "power" (*kratos*). In themselves, elections are not democracy; they are a way in which democracy—rule by the people—can be expressed. By the same token, elections that do not give ordinary people some power are a travesty of democracy.

The point is not a terminological nicety. In Central America, as we have noted, the power that counts has been held by tiny oligarchical elites and the military. *They are not voted in—and they cannot be voted out.* Even when votes are counted honestly, the power of the elites and the military cannot be threatened by electoral politics. For the most part in Central America, serious reform proposals do not enter party politics. That has certainly been the case in Guatemala since the CIA-organized coup in 1954. When political parties or candidates do make such proposals, they are thwarted through bribery, fraud, or coercion. Notable examples are the electoral frauds in El Salvador in 1972 and 1977. If all else fails, the military coup always remains an option.

In a word, elections do not create democracy—rather, a valid democracy can be expressed through elections.

All this is emphatically true of El Salvador. Since 1979 the most important item on the government's agenda has been the defeat of the left, and that is primarily the task of the army and security forces. To a degree, the United States, which supplies at least 30 to 40 percent of the government's budget, has supplanted the oligarchy as the military's partner. Ultimately, what the Salvadoran government and armed forces are defending is no longer the oligarchy as such but U.S. hegemony. Elections have played a critical role in giving the government a semblance of legitimacy. However, the oligarchy and military, who resent U.S. impositions, have fought back through the ARENA party, which is the political expression of the groups who organized the death squads.

In May 1984, José Napoleón Duarte achieved his lifelong ambition of becoming president of El Salvador. An uncritical U.S. Congress hastened to provide the Reagan administration with $70 million more in military aid and $135 million in economic aid. Few pointed out that 15,000 civilians had been killed by security forces during Duarte's previous term as president of the junta. Although his election seemed to promise diplomatic initiatives on the part of El Salvador, in fact, Duarte emphasized in his inaugural address that he would negotiate with the FMLN only after it had laid down its arms. Surrender was the precondition to negotiations. In no way did Duarte's election represent democracy in the sense of the people having power. His power—even with the support of the Salvadoran military—comes from the United States and from his usefulness as a legitimizing presence. That he is personally sincere and upright is irrelevant—or even dangerous to the extent his election lubricates the U.S. slide toward deeper military involvement. Duarte's ultimate role in history may be to appeal to the United States to invade El Salvador in order to "save" a "democracy" of its own making.

In Guatemala, the army continues as the real arbiter of national affairs—through the electoral fraud and subsequent coup of 1982, the coup of 1983, and the elections leading toward a constituent assembly in 1984, which should prepare for elections in 1985. Although it may allow some civilian participation, the army will continue to define the parameters and will tolerate no civilian threat to its own power.

Between 1979 and 1981, Honduras moved back toward formal democracy and civilian rule, but in fact General Álvarez (and U.S. ambassador John Negroponte) made the essential decisions, sometimes without even consulting with the Honduran congress. The military coup of April 1984 signified not a return to democracy, but a shift from Álvarez's personal rule to a more collective control by the military top command.

Even on a formal and procedural level the election held in Nicaragua in November 1984 compares favorably with those held in neighboring countries. While in El Salvador the ballots were transparent and were put into transparent boxes, giving many voters the sense that their choices could be observed, in Nicaragua the ballots were put into wooden boxes. The voting procedure was simple and the vote count clean. There was nothing like the degree of coercion that existed in El Salvador, where citizens were required to have their identity papers stamped at the polling place. There was no climate of murder such as exists in El Salvador and Guatemala.

In the United States much attention was focused on the candidacy of Arturo Cruz, who was portrayed as the moderate opposition figure. When he finally refused to participate—after four separate periods of negotiation with the Sandinistas—the U.S. media tended to regard the election as insignificant. The media seemed not to notice that within Nicaragua, Cruz was not a popular figure. He had spent most of the previous fifteen years outside Nicaragua, working in international banking institutions. He was the candidate of the business and upper-class sectors, who have opposed the Sandinista revolution almost from the beginning. It is quite possible that the whole Cruz candidacy was primarily a ploy in the overall destabilization strategy.

Critics pointed out that with their control of the government and with their own mass organizations the Sandinistas had an advantage over the other parties. Yet honest observers agreed that the Sandinistas would win fair elections. The election may be viewed, then, as a plebiscite of sorts, and as a mechanism for institutionalizing the revolution, including the admission of a minority participation in the government by opposition parties.

Can such elections be regarded as democratic? If democracy is taken to be synonymous with the two-party or multiparty systems of government of Europe or North America, the answer is clearly no. However, if the resulting government can be said to be really responsive to the people and to provide the majority with meaningful participation and a share in real power, then they might be called democratic.

Historically, revolutionary governments have tended to come to the point where they believe their programs are synonymous with the will of the people. Thus criticism itself tends to be regarded as bordering on treason. The presence of a real opposition in Nicaragua—within the overall revolutionary process—could help keep the revolution and the Sandinistas honest. If the Sandinistas were to develop a form of electoral democracy compatible with revolutionary transformation, it might constitute a real innovation. Here, however, the argument is modest: it is simply that the Sandinista election is more democratic in the root sense of the word than those of El Salvador, Honduras, and Guatemala, and that it should not be rejected out of hand.

In considering the issue of democracy in Central America, the focus should be primarily on function, not simply on forms and mechanisms. The question is whether ordinary people, the poor majority, participate in a meaningful way in public life and in the decisions that affect them. Appropriate forms for a functional democracy may require experimentation—even the experimentation of a revolution like Nicaragua's.

Economic Development

In 1982, the Reagan administration unveiled its Caribbean Basin Initiative, dubbed a "mini–Marshall Plan" because of its ambitious scope. One-third of the Kissinger Commission report was made up of proposals for economic and human development. The overall price tag was $24 billion, $8 billion of it to be supplied by the United States by 1989.

The most obvious response to such a grandiose proposal is that in an era of dangerous U.S. budget deficits, it is highly unrealistic. Its effect—whether consciously planned or not—is to sugarcoat a bitter military pill. Nevertheless, the notion of "saving" Central America through economic development deserves some brief comment, since it does have a surface appeal.

First, the underlying economic diagnosis of the Kissinger Commission report is misleading. It presents the crisis as deriving primarily from the rise in oil prices and the world recession (entailing declining prices for Central America's raw materials), as well as increased government borrowing combined with higher interest rates. All these factors have seriously aggravated the crisis—but it existed even when growth rates, as measured in conventional terms, were quite high. The very development model that brought such growth also brought deteriorating standards of living (see pp. 15–20).

In addition, the report fails to differentiate between countries. Genuine development is impossible under the war conditions prevailing in El Salvador and Guatemala. Moreover, the U.S. determination to subordinate Honduras and Costa Rica to its own geostrategic purposes is preventing them from adequately dealing with their own financial and development problems. Nicaragua's participation will be blocked until it changes its behavior—despite the fact that development for the poor is a serious part of the government agenda only in Nicaragua and Costa Rica.

While the economic recommendations of the Kissinger report could help governments weather the present international recession, genuine development (development that will affect a majority of the people of Central America) will take place only if there is a political solution to the crisis, and if governments are able to begin reforms that are structural—that is, reforms that begin to modify the model of development.

These are some of the common themes of the debate on Central America in the United States. The overall aim has been to move from a U.S.-centered and ethnocentric discussion in order that some of these issues might be seen from the perspective of those most affected: ordinary Central Americans.

As noted initially, much of the debate is misplaced in that it fails to grasp that the core of the policy has been essentially military. Crucial questions remain: Will this policy work? Where is it leading us?

FOUR

CONFRONTING REVOLUTION: OUTCOMES

As early as 1980 some people intuited that the United States was headed toward a Vietnam-like involvement in Central America, and that seemed more likely as time went on. One could even set out the implicit logic in syllogistic form:

1. United States policy in Central America is aimed at overthrowing the Sandinista government (or forcing it to change so thoroughly that it is no longer revolutionary) and at defeating insurgency in El Salvador (and Guatemala).
2. However, these aims cannot be realized with the present level of means—that is, funding and organizing the anti-Sandinista *contras*, and propping up the Salvadoran army and government.
3. Therefore, the United States will have to either escalate its means (including eventually sending U.S. combat personnel) or revise its aims (that is, accept negotiated settlements).

The specter of a direct U.S. invasion loomed high during 1983–1984, and many believed it was almost inevitable during a second Reagan term in office. By early 1985, however, it seemed possible that the Reagan administration was recognizing the high political costs of such an invasion.

The overthrow of the Sandinistas and the military defeat of the FMLN remained the preferred outcome. However, the administration might be willing to accept a less satisfactory but still tolerable outcome, namely, a policy of military attack, economic strangulation, and diplomatic isolation that would force the Sandinista revolution to put all its energies into survival, and enough military and economic aid to El Salvador to prevent either an FMLN victory or a negotiated settlement on terms favorable to the FMLN-FDR.

It seemed possible, in other words, that the administration might be willing to pursue this second outcome, "containment," for some time, while not completely abandoning the aim of eventually achieving the preferred and more decisive outcome, "rollback." The hardliners would continue to lobby for decisive military solutions, while the moderates would insist that a single-minded pursuit of victory in Central America might endanger other aspects of the Reagan program.

This chapter is concerned with the foreseeable results of pursuing either of these outcomes: the probability of direct U.S. intervention implicit in "rollback," and the high human cost and uncertain consequences of "containment."

RESULTS OF CURRENT U.S. POLICIES

Nicaragua

Since the advent of the Reagan administration, the basic objective of policy toward Nicaragua has been the overthrow of the Sandinistas, occasional pro forma denials to the contrary notwithstanding. Certainly the aim of the *contras* has never been to "interdict" arms being shipped to El Salvador.

In 1981 and 1982, the *contras* and their U.S. enthusiasts seem to have believed in the possibility of establishing a beachhead in the sparsely populated eastern region of Nicaragua. By then declaring this a "free territory," they would give their movement some legitimacy and open the way for international recognition by various governments.

However, most Nicaraguans viewed the *contras* as both a continuation of *somocismo* (the word denotes the whole Somoza system) and as one more example of U.S. "imperialism," which has a history stretching from William Walker in the 1850s through two decades of U.S. Marine occupation of their country in this century, as well as interventions in Guatemala, Cuba, the Dominican Republic, and Chile. The behavior of the *contras*—torturing, raping, and killing civilians, as well as attacking cooperatives, health centers, and schools—reinforced that interpretation. Furthermore, the United

States overestimated the anti-Somoza credentials of Edén Pastora. Despite his previous fame, he was perceived as a traitor by many Nicaraguans when he took up arms against the Sandinistas. His ignominy was complete by 1984, when his links to the CIA were revealed, despite his frequent diatribes against the CIA.

By September 1983, there were indications that U.S. policymakers had concluded that the *contra* would not ignite any anti-Sandinista rebellion. Tactics shifted toward more direct attacks on the Nicaraguan economy. Fuel storage facilities were blown up and harbors were mined. Even the pretense of an internal revolt was lost when the press revealed that those responsible were CIA "Latino assets"—that is, Latin American mercenaries and not Nicaraguans.

United States strategy then aimed at strangling the Nicaraguan revolution through sabotage, continued *contra* raids, blocking development loans from international banks, and isolating Nicaragua diplomatically. The hope was perhaps that as life become more difficult the Nicaraguan people would blame the Sandinistas and then be ripe either to revolt themselves or to welcome a "liberating" army. The first difficulty with this strategy is that it is so obvious and simply illustrates what the Sandinistas say about "imperialism." In response, the Sandinistas have shifted to a survival economy, placing priority on self-sufficiency in basic foods (corn and beans), and maintaining programs in health, education, and agriculture that have benefitted the poor majority. To do so, they have postponed more ambitious development projects, but they have also curtailed luxury imports. Consequently, those whose standard of living has been most affected by the added austerity measures, the middle and upper classes, are the natural allies of the *contras* and the United States. Some middle-class people might angrily rally behind the Sandinistas while others might seek to leave the country. In any case, the constituency for counterrevolution is undermined. Such a plan could make sense only if it succeeded in so wearying the Nicaraguan people that they would have little will to resist an attack led by the United States under a suitable pretext.

Sometimes U.S. policy is justified as "pressure" to induce the Sandinistas to modify their behavior—for example, to stop supporting other revolutionary movements. However, in late 1983, the Sandinistas did a number of things that seemed to respond to stated U.S. objectives. Some Cubans and members of Central American revolutionary groups left the country, press censorship was lightened, and elections were announced. These moves were dismissed as insignificant or as proof that "pressure" was working and should be increased. However, as flexible as the Sandinistas might be on particular issues, no amount of pressure will make them renounce the overall aim of carrying out revolutionary changes. What the Reagan administration seems to find most offensive is not particular policies but the audacity of attempting a revolution in what the United States has regarded as its "backyard."

In short, present U.S. policies will neither overthrow the Sandinistas nor force them to change so much that they become tolerable to the present administration—that is, nonrevolutionary.

El Salvador

In early 1985, after almost five years of deepening U.S. military involvement in El Salvador, government forces were nowhere near victory. Guerrilla forces had shown an ability to adapt to continual isolation.

In 1977, El Salvador had rejected U.S. military aid rather than be subject to human rights criteria. In 1979 and 1980, the Carter administration moved to renew military aid—even though the rate of security force and death-squad murders was a hundred times what it had been when the aid was cut off. The opening wedge was the introduction of "nonlethal" riot-control gear (over the protests of Archbishop Romero, who said the aid would be used against the people). The U.S.-supplied equipment that followed included communications equipment, trucks and jeeps, uniforms and personal equipment, weapons and ammunition of all kinds, helicopters, transport planes, and fighters.

With the rebel offensive of early 1981, the Carter administration approved the sending of the first military advisors. The Reagan administration soon raised their number from 35 to 55, and later stretched the figure by reclassifying some military personnel in El Salvador and basing others in Honduras, from which they could commute to El Salvador by plane.

Once the Salvadoran army's equipment had been modernized, the key element became training. U.S. advisors could see that the Salvadoran army was not made for fighting. They trained an elite rapid-reaction batallion and, as time went on, trained more. They also set about reorganizing the army, starting at the very top and working their way down to where they were directing the prosecution of the war.

The Salvadoran officer corps has been a constant problem. Historically, the main purpose of Central American armies has been repression, not combat. In El Salvador an officer's key to advancement and spoils has been his *tanda*, or graduating class in the military academy, and loyalty to the *tanda* has been a first principle. There is little tradition of advancement through merit.

U.S. military advisors and diplomats complained aloud that the officers had a nine-to-five mentality toward combat and were unwilling to change their methods—for example, by operating in small patrols and undertaking night missions. Few officers were willing to risk their lives, as the very low number of officers killed in battle indicated. U.S. strategists concluded that the officer corps had to be purged so that younger U.S.-trained officers could move up in the ranks. The retirement of the defense minister, Colonel Guillermo García, in April 1983 paved the way for the further Americanization of the war, although the officer corps proved resistant.

One example of this Americanization was the National Plan for the provinces of San Vicente and Usulután in 1983, modeled after pacification plans in Vietnam. The army was to rid the area of guerrillas and then remain to oversee a series of civic action programs that would "win hearts and minds." The guerrillas indeed dispersed initially, and the program was taken to be a success. After a few months, however, it became clear that guerrillas still controlled areas of the provinces and that U.S.-funded schools and clinics functioned only with their approval.

This development was but one illustration of a general tendency. For every new threshhold of U.S. involvement, for every increase in expenditure, for every expansion of the Salvadoran armed forces, the insurgency seemed to more than compensate. Although the 1981 general offensive failed to spark a Nicaragua-like insurrection, the FMLN did extend its control over a significant amount of territory and was able to continue its attacks. By early 1983, it had taken the town of Berlin; and in September of that year, it took San Miguel, the third largest city in the country. That several hundred combatants, some carrying mortars, had been able to surprise the army argues for considerable support among the peasantry. On December

30, the FMLN destroyed the army base at Paraíso, designed by U.S. army engineers to be impregnable. They inflicted so many casualties that the Salvadoran army had to bury the bodies with bulldozers.

Having concluded that the situation of the Salvadoran army was so serious that "a collapse is not inconceivable," the Kissinger Commission advocated an extra $400 million in military aid during the following year and a half. They urged that funding be "multiyear," presumably to assure the Salvadoran military of U.S. reliability.

In early 1984, under U.S. direction, the Salvadoran military moved toward an air-war strategy. Information from U.S. surveillance missions was used to monitor guerrilla movements, and rapid-reaction units were flown by helicopter into areas of rebel movement. Bombing was increased, and the overall aim seemed to be to drive the civilian population out of FMLN-held territory. This air-war strategy became even more clear when the United States delivered the first AC-47 gunships to El Salvador and when it was announced that by the end of 1985 the Salvadoran military would have 49 helicopters.

Once again U.S. military advisors and embassy personnel began to speak in optimistic terms, noting that the rhythm of FMLN activity had diminished and it had not carried out spectacular actions. What was more likely was that it was adjusting its strategy to the new circumstances. The FMLN claimed to have inflicted 2,030 casualties from June through September 1984. It was able to mount a major attack on the city of Suchitoto without its movements being detected. The rebels had expanded their operations into twelve of El Salvador's fourteen provinces, and there were indications that they planned to mount new activity in the urban areas. In attacking the *masas*, peasants judged to be supporting the FMLN, the military may have hoped to copy the Guatemalan success, but there were real constraints since human-rights organizations, the international press, and the Catholic Church were drawing attention both to mass killings and to bombing of civilians.

There is no reason to believe that the fundamental difficulty of the Salvadoran army can be solved by any amount of U.S. aid, training, equipment, or advice. It is what the United States itself recognizes as a "morale problem." Casualty rates have continued to grow, as have surrenders. Between December 1983 and May 1984 alone, over 1,000 government troops surrendered to the insurgents. By taking prisoners, the FMLN received weapons, some recruits, and much good will. It turned prisoners over to the International Red Cross to protect them against retaliation, in marked contrast to the Salvadoran army's practice of killing prisoners. Another indication of the low morale was that only 10 percent of the U.S.-trained noncommissioned officers were re-enlisting at the end of their two-year tours of duty.

A moment's reflection on the situation of the ordinary Salvadoran soldier will help clarify the morale problem. That soldier was probably press-ganged into service. He is aware that some army officers are profiteering (even by selling weapons and ammunition to the FMLN) and that most of the civilians killed (including perhaps his own friends and relatives) are victims of the official forces. Deep down he is probably also aware that Americans are directing the war ultimately for their own purposes. Furthermore, should the insurgents win, the oligarchy and the top military officers would resume their lives in Miami or elsewhere with money taken out of El Salvador. Ultimately he is expected to risk his life for the sake of continued U.S. domination of its "backyard." The ordinary Salvadoran soldier or officer has nothing worth dying for. His most reasonable goal in such a situation is personal survival. No amount of U.S. aid, equipment, advice, or training is likely to change that reality.

U.S. strategy in El Salvador underestimates the political dimension of the situation as well. From the counterinsurgency perspective, the primary aim is the military defeat of the insurgents. Political programs are aimed simply at "winning hearts and minds" away from the insurgents and are used in combination with repression. The country's basic problems are fundamentally ignored. The Salvadoran government has little to offer its people but repression. Moreover, there are sharp divisions within the government and military between those who accept some U.S. impositions like land reform or feeble limits on death-squad activity and those who resent any U.S. conditions and are convinced that subversion is ended by killing those whom they label subversives. It is important to see that political disputes are not simply the product of personal ambitions, but of genuine contradictions within the power structure. That local politicians resist U.S. pressures might appear to refute the charge that they are puppets. Actually, what it shows is that, as in Vietnam, they are bad puppets.

Insurgent forces, which view the struggle as fundamentally political, can take advantage of the contradictions inherent in the government's policies. For example, government policies such as a freeze on wage increases and the enactment of new indirect taxes to pay for the war (rather than increasing taxes on property and income) have reduced people's buying power. In order to defend themselves, people have defied government violence and sometimes organized strikes. Even nonleftist labor unions end up in conflict with the government. During the 1984 electoral period, for example, some 40,000 people went on strike. The primary reason was that inflation had continued to reduce real wages. One of the demands of striking postal workers was simply that the government supply them with shoes and uniforms, which had become prohibitively expensive.

For U.S. strategists, the political dimension of the overall counterinsurgency effort was apparently limited to managing the election of José Napoleón Duarte. By contrast, the FMLN-FDR no doubt saw the government's inability to deal with the basic needs of the population—and the people's spontaneous efforts to defend their rights—as primary political facts.

In early 1985 the administration seemed optimistic about the direction of the war in El Salvador. There was little evidence, however, that the Salvadoran military was near victory.

DIRECT U.S. INTERVENTION

Any responsible assessment of the thrust of U.S. policy must consider the consequences of direct combat involvement, even though it involves a degree of speculation.

Nicaragua

Many saw in the U.S. invasion of Grenada in October 1983 a model for possible action against Nicaragua. That troops from several small neighboring countries accompanied U.S. forces provided a semblance of legitimacy. Domestically, the invasion was a political plus. Many Americans seemed proud that their country had scored a "success," after what they had seen as humiliation by Third World radicals. Administration representatives were content to let others, including the Sandinistas, draw their own conclusions about U.S. willingness to use direct military force. In subsequent weeks and months, Nicaraguans began to intensify their preparations for defense against attack.

Nicaragua, however, is not Grenada. It has over 400 times the territory and 20 times the population. Moreover, it has an army of 30,000, and its militia may number as many as 200,000. The revolution is the product of a broad-based armed insurrection.

Should the United States (and its regional allies) strike with a large attack force, it could, after hard fighting, probably take and occupy Managua and the larger towns. It would then be an occupation army. Even if it could install a civilian government, it would face a large and determined guerrilla army that would operate freely throughout most of the country. The Sandinistas have made contingency plans for fighting such a war, including the caching of arms and ammunition. Furthermore, many Sandinista sympathizers would remain in the towns, and simply to weed them out, an occupation army would have to carry out political repression far worse than that of the Pinochet regime in Chile after the 1973 coup. Those who elected to work with the Americans would be viewed by most of the Nicaraguan people as collaborators. The result could only be a murderous and insecure police state.

Sandinista confidence in ultimate victory would be bolstered by the memory of Augusto César Sandino, whom the U.S. Marines had been unable to defeat a half century before. To satisfy the collaborators, the United States might undo Sandinista advances in land reform, further alienating the population. It could not continue the Sandinista health and education programs in their present form since they depend on the very grassroots organizations it would be trying to dismantle. Hence, it is hard to imagine how any government installed under the U.S. occupation army could attain legitimacy, even through "free elections." Before undertaking an invasion of Nicaragua, policymakers should ask themselves not only how the United States could occupy Nicaragua but, more importantly, how it could leave.

One assumes that such considerations must give pause even to enthusiastic military strategists and those itching to roll back what they see as Marxist gains.

Caution in the face of such considerations might lead planners to scale down their proposals to simply U.S. bombing attacks. Undoubtedly, in two days of bombing the United States could destroy much of the Nicaraguan economy and the main military installations. However, history (most recently in Vietnam) shows that bombing normally steels a population to defend its homeland.

El Salvador

Large-scale direct U.S. military intervention might seem more feasible in El Salvador than in Nicaragua for several reasons. The "enemy" numbers only 6,000 (though some reports contend 10,000) guerrillas and presently occupies a relatively small territory. An appeal for help from an "elected" government and participation by neighboring armies might provide the appearance of legitimacy.

A U.S. invasion to defeat the insurgency could include intense bombing, followed by a massive infantry sweep through guerrilla strongholds. For domestic reasons, a U.S. administration would strive to avoid the appearance of being bogged down in El Salvador. Thus, it would try to carry out an operation that would permit a swift U.S. withdrawal, perhaps before Congress could compel one under the War Powers Act. The aim would be a quick success, with little loss of U.S. life.

However, miscalculation is highly probable. The FMLN also has contingency plans for a U.S. invasion, which it sees as almost certain. Inevitably, the United States would find itself making war on the civilian population as the FMLN split into small units. The FMLN would probably adopt a strategy of wearing down an army of occupation, greatly increasing the political cost in the United States. Faced with political pressures to withdraw, the United States would yet know that if it did, the FMLN could regroup and continue.

Far from being solved, El Salvador's underlying problems would be aggravated by a U.S. occupation army. The economy would become more distorted and artificial, and corruption would be expanded with the new opportunities provided by massive amounts of U.S. money and personnel. What had been a struggle against a local oligarchy would become a war of national liberation.

THE LOGIC OF REGIONALIZATION

Since 1981, Central Americans have spoken of the "regionalization" of conflicts—that is, the spreading of local conflicts. The clearest example of this can be seen in Honduras. It has been brought into neighboring conflicts by harboring and supporting the *contras*, carrying out joint operations with the Salvadoran army, sometimes engaging in combat inside El Salvador, and allowing a massive U.S. military buildup on its territory. Regionalization is already a reality.

In the sense intended here, however, regionalization is a kind of underlying logic by which direct U.S. military intervention in one country will spread to others.

This might happen in several ways. For example, if the United States were to become bogged down in combat in El Salvador, policymakers might insist on going "to the source" and attacking Nicaragua. However, if Nicaragua were attacked as part of an overall effort to defeat revolutionary forces in the region, the Sandinistas might very well conclude that the battleground included all Central America and see no further reason to restrict their support of other revolutionary movements.

If the United States forms a regional coalition of armies (including those of Honduras, El Salvador, and, conceivably, Guatemala) why should the revolutionary organizations not do something similar? Why should they not help Honduran dissident groups turn to revolutionary war both for their own cause and out of solidarity? Moreover, they might carry out terrorist-style attacks on U.S. personnel and installations.

Guatemala should not be forgotten either. Until late 1981, the Guatemalan insurgency seemed to be making impressive advances. At that point, the army retook the initiative with its policy of mass killings in Indian villages suspected of guerrilla sympathies, but the Guatemalan revolutionary movement cannot be discounted. The army has been loathe to become closely identified with U.S. regional operations because it faces a serious guerrilla threat at home. If the overall logic of regionalization drew the Guatemalan army into conflict, the United States eventually might find itself at war in Guatemala as well.

Even Costa Rica cannot be utterly excluded. The country is in a serious financial crisis, and the population has suffered a severe drop in its standard of living. From 1977 to 1982 the number of families living below the government-defined poverty line jumped from 24 percent to 71 percent—almost half the population. This crisis is structural and may signal a breakdown of the economic model Costa Rica has followed since the late 1940s. Any shortsighted U.S. efforts to press the Costa Rican government into its regional strategy will increase the likelihood that Costa Rican elites will deal not with the causes of the crisis but with its effects—through repression. Costa Rica's fate might be like that of Uruguay—another small, prosperous, middle-class democracy that in the mid-1970s was rapidly

transformed into a nation with the highest per capita number of political prisoners in the world. The repression of people's legitimate
efforts to defend their rights would heighten unrest and could at
some point lead to a serious revolutionary movement in Costa Rica.

POLITICAL AND DIPLOMATIC CONSEQUENCES

United States government representatives have repeatedly stated
that there are "no intentions" of sending U.S. troops into combat in
Central America. (The countermessage is that one "never says
'never.'") The one element that could make Central America a key
concern for ordinary citizens is U.S. combat deaths.

Direct intervention by the United States would propel the present
anti-intervention movement into a full-scale antiwar movement. It
would be reminiscent of the Vietnam era but also different. Such an
antiwar movement would not be primarily a youth movement, and
particularly, it would not be confused with a cultural revolution. It
would not be campus-based, but rather would reach into mainstream institutions, such as the churches and labor unions, and from
the beginning would enjoy the respectability provided by prominent
citizens and political leaders.

Church leaders, both Catholic and Protestant, have spoken repeatedly against military solutions and in favor of negotiated approaches (in this, echoing what church leaders in Central America
have advocated). Direct U.S. intervention would move the churches
from pronouncements to much more organized opposition, and possibly toward active support of civil disobedience.

Many of the nation's Hispanics—about 10 percent of the population—would identify with the people against whom such a war was
being waged, and many U.S. soldiers would be Hispanics and
blacks. Minority communities might join demonstrations as well,
seeing both a war being waged on other poor people and the continued decay of their own communities.

Clearly, a United States intervention in Central America would in
all probability fuel a militant antiwar movement running through
the entire society.

Protest would not be restricted to the United States either. The
worldwide indignation over the mining of Nicaraguan ports can give
only a hint of the international impact of a U.S. invasion. An "Amer-

ican Afghanistan" would certainly fuel the European peace movements and make even more appealing the notion that Europe should pursue its own international policies, especially vis-à-vis the Eastern bloc. European political leaders, whatever their own ideas, might find it increasingly difficult to support U.S. objectives in NATO.

Furthermore, U.S. diplomats might be surprised to find Latin American countries (except for the U.S.'s Central American allies) united in repudiating a U.S. intervention. Consistently, the United States has spurned Mexico's advice and negotiating efforts. A U.S. invasion would rub salt in old wounds left over from the Monroe Doctrine.

Finally, we should mention costs. One researcher has estimated that even a military victory in El Salvador without U.S. combat troops would cost some $7 billion between 1984 and 1989. A scenario that included an invasion of Nicaragua, even if successful, would cost $16 billion. In reality, the figures would probably run much higher. For example, it is assumed that a U.S. force of only 25,000 combat troops could defeat the Sandinistas, a calculation that seems to underestimate the strength of the Sandinista army and militia, as well as the impact of Nicaraguans' knowledge of their country and their motivation to defend it. By contrast, a negotiated solution, including subsequent economic aid, would probably cost around $4 billion.

THE COSTS OF CONTAINMENT

If the projections just made have any validity, even those who are ideologically inclined to pursue a decisive military victory might be forced to accept something less. In effect, the United States might simply "draw the line" in Central America by continuing to follow its present policies indefinitely, regardless of the impact on Central Americans themselves.

If the United States cannot expel the Sandinistas without invading, it can still do all in its power to make the revolution fail. By mid-1984, over 2,700 Nicaraguans had been killed by the *contras*, and several thousand more had been wounded or abducted. Those especially targeted were government workers, teachers, and lay church leaders. Much of the 1984–1985 coffee crop could not be picked because of a deliberate *contra* policy of attacking coffee pickers and installations. Damage done by the *contras* that year was estimated at $254.9 million, or an amount equivalent to 70 percent of Nicaragua's export revenues.

In response to these attacks and to U.S. threats, the Sandinista government planned to spend 40 percent of its 1985 budget on defense. Those resources were thereby made unavailable for development. In fact, the Sandinistas were being forced to give up more ambitious long-term development projects. The United States was increasingly seeking to strangle Nicaragua economically by cutting off sources of credit and closing off markets. It used its weight in the World Bank and the Inter-American Development Bank to block loans to Nicaragua, even to the point of angering some member countries, who objected to the politicization of these institutions.

If Nicaragua is forced to put all its energies into sheer survival, it will have no chance of finding new and appropriate solutions to the problem of development. People may accept the need to defend their country, but they will see little material betterment in their lives. Nicaragua will scarcely be able to provide a model for any other country to emulate. Moreover, if the Sandinistas take authoritarian measures or if they seek closer economic ties to the socialist block, they will thereby appear to validate all the criticisms leveled at them.

In early 1985 it seemed that U.S. strategy in El Salvador was heavily dependent on the air war. Apparently the overall aim was to attack the FMLN-controlled areas so thoroughly that the guerrillas' civilian base of support would disappear. The attacks were also aimed at "disputed" areas, that is, those zones where neither the army nor the FMLN had a permanent presence, so as to prevent any potential future support for the guerrillas. At the same time, the United States was preparing to increase its spending on refugee relief, and there was talk that the Salvadoran refugees in Honduras would be repatriated into western El Salvador. Such ostensibly humanitarian aid would in reality be an integral part of an overall counterinsurgency plan.

In this containment scheme, Honduras becomes a kind of South Korea, a bulwark of U.S. military strength to deter any further expansion of hostile forces. Thus the U.S. military bases and exercises become a permanent feature in Honduras.

Viewing it superficially, some Americans might find such containment attractive. When compared with the prospect of direct U.S. invasion, it might even seem a moderate course. U.S. aims—the halting of leftist advance in Central America—would be achieved at apparently little cost.

That, however, is an illusion. Simply continuing present policies in this fashion might soon cost a billion dollars a year. For the 1986 fiscal year, the Reagan administration was asking Congress to approve $483 million in aid for El Salvador.

Moreover, the real cost is being borne by Central Americans. Thousands of people are killed each year; living standards continue to decline; in fact, the whole social fabric of Central America is being destroyed. One-tenth of the population of El Salvador is already uprooted and displaced, and the air war will drive more people from their homes.

Under such a containment policy, Central America would become a permanent crisis area. Perhaps Americans might come to believe that violence was simply a inescapable fact in Central America, something endemic to the region, and that no solution was possible.

However, there is no guarantee that in the long run U.S. interests would be served. There is reason to doubt that even with air power the Salvadoran military would prevail, given the understandable lack of motivation noted earlier. A little-noticed episode in early December 1984 seems to bear out this assessment. In the village of El Salto, near the town of Zacatecoluca, a U.S.-trained rapid-reaction battalion of 350 men ran into a larger guerrilla force and suffered heavy casualties. Even though the sounds of the battle could be heard in Zacatecoluca for seven hours, no help was sent, nor was help sent from San Salvador until a day and a half later. A U.S. journalist who visited El Salto concluded that the tactics and capabilities of the guerrillas did not "appear to be those of a weak, demoralized foe" and that "doubts about the Salvadoran army will persist."

The logic of either rollback or containment will lead to disaster, either that of a direct U.S. invasion or that of a continual bleeding of Central America. It is this logic that impelled the leaders of the Contadora countries—Mexico, Venezuela, Colombia, and Panama—to begin pressing for negotiated solutions. These governments range from moderate to conservative, but they are convinced that a protracted and possibly regional war close to them threatens their own interests.

Before discussing negotiation proposals, however, we must face a prior question: Can the United States deal with revolutionary movements at all?

FIVE

THE UNITED STATES AND CENTRAL AMERICAN REVOLUTIONS: IS ANY ACCOMMODATION POSSIBLE?

The alternative to the present policies, which are aimed at militarily defeating revolutionary movements, must be the kind of political approach advocated by many governments. Implicit in such an approach is the possibility that leftist governments might emerge in Central America as they have in Africa—for example, internationally supervised elections in Rhodesia-Zimbabwe led to a Marxist government (which the conservative Thatcher government in Britian has successfully lived with).

Such a possibility represents the major stumbling block for the United States. Even congressional critics of administration policy hasten to insist that the advent of more leftist governments in Latin America would signify defeat for the United States.

The underlying question in considering negotiated approaches is whether revolutionary movements threaten U.S. security and are incompatible with U.S. interests.

SECURITY THREATS

The most persistent justification for U.S. policy in Central America has been that revolutionary governments or movements there jeopardize U.S. security. The assumption is that these movements are connected to the Soviet Union through Cuba and that their taking power must represent a victory for the USSR and a defeat for the United States.

Arguments along the following lines are often advanced:

1. Nicaragua, backed by Cuba, is already supporting subversion in neighboring countries; other revolutionary governments would only extend subversion and widen the threat.

2. Revolutionary governments in Central America linked to the Soviet Union and Cuba would force the United States for the first time to deploy defense forces to protect its southern flank, thus reducing its ability to project its power elsewhere in the world.

3. U.S. sea lanes in the Caribbean and the Panama Canal would be made more vulnerable by additional revolutionary governments in the region. Even now, the USSR has a greater capacity to interdict U.S. shipping than did the Nazis.

4. Communist takeovers will send a tidal wave of refugees to the United States, reaching perhaps into the millions, putting even greater pressure on U.S. jobs and communities.

5. Finally, there is the question of credibility. If the United States cannot prevail in an area as close as Central America, its ability to influence events elsewhere in the world will be impaired.

The first point is perhaps the most crucial insofar as it involves the nature of revolution itself and how revolution occurs. Some use physical analogies—"dominoes," "cancer," "prairie fire"—that emphasize geographical contiguity. Secretary of State Haig spoke of a Soviet "hit list" as though the course of all revolutions were determined from the Kremlin. Those who see revolution as the result of small conspiratorial groups assiduously trace connections to a worldwide terrorist network.

Revolution, however, does not occur as a result of the handiwork of a conspiratorial elite. Rather, it begins when social change—indeed, social breakdown—is affecting large numbers of people, so that they become committed to struggle, and when the power structure is weakened or delegitimized. (We are, of course, speaking of genuine revolutions and not barracks coups.) Revolutionary organizations have an undeniable role, but by themselves they cannot create revolutions.

In Chapters 1 and 2 we noted that revolutionary conditions did appear in El Salvador, Guatemala, and Nicaragua; and revolutionary organizations arose as well. However, for other nations in the region, this is not the case. Such conditions did not appear in Honduras and Costa Rica, nor have they to this day. Ordinary Costa Ricans feel they have a stake in their society because their economy and the government's social welfare programs have worked for most people. Relatively speaking, Costa Rican egalitarianism and prosperity are deeply rooted because ordinary farmers shared in the coffee prosperity of the nineteenth century. In Honduras the oligarchy appeared late and is underdeveloped; moreover, the country's relative underpopulation means that Honduran peasants have access to more land than do those in El Salvador. In principle, Honduras and Costa Rica could deal with their development problems in an evolutionary, reformist way. To the extent U.S. policy militarizes them, however, it will be cutting off avenues for peaceful change. Should that happen, revolutionary conditions could indeed develop, especially in Honduras.

Structurally, Panama is the most unrevolutionary country in Latin America. It is not primarily an agroexport country; its economy revolves around its "transit function"—the canal, the free zone, and U.S. military bases. Since the 1960s, it has become a leading finance center, with foreign deposits far outstripping domestic deposits. Today, Panama's economic stability depends on its remaining a safe haven for foreign depositors and for the many "paper" companies incorporated there. The slightest hint of genuine instability would deplete its banks. It was perhaps this underlying structural requirement for stability that enabled General Torrijos (1968–1982) to flirt with rhetorical revolution. In practice his programs were no more than populist. Panama cannot afford to become revolutionary, no matter what happens to other countries in the region. Furthermore, any terrorists wishing to destroy the canal locks could do so today from Panama itself with no need of a revolutionary country as a springboard.

Some people fear that Mexico's extremes of wealth and poverty make it a potential revolutionary target. It is true that Mexico's development has left large numbers of people, especially peasants and Indians in the south, in poverty. However, Mexico has a diversified economy and its population of 70 million is spread over a large territory in which conditions vary widely. Even though the present economic crisis affects all, its impact is different in the slums of Mexico City, the border towns of the north, and the coastal tropical areas. Until now the Mexican army has suppressed occasional peasant unrest, while most of the population remained unaware. If an economic crisis were to affect people everywhere in a drastic way, and if organizers could create a unified national movement, something like a revolution might occur. That, however, would be a result of internal conditions. Revolution in Central America would be only a distant influence. It should be noted that the Mexican government's good relations with Cuba over the last twenty-five years—it was the only Latin American government that refused to follow the U.S. lead in breaking relations—have had no appreciable spillover into domestic politics.

Other governments in the region, such as Colombia, Venezuela, and Panama, do not see leftist governments in Central America as a threat to their security. They understand revolutions to be the product of particular social circumstances and organized movements; they do not need to drag in misleading physical analogies and notions of international intrigue.

Those who focus on the security threat tend to see revolutionaries as part of a monolithic global communist movement. In fact, however, revolutionary organizations vary greatly among themselves. Many, if not most, Marxists are independent of Moscow. The Central American revolutionaries are, by and large, Marxists but they do not link their fates to the Soviet Union. This is partly a result of their experience and partly a function of their nationalistic ideology. In other words, they want to be nonaligned.

The notion that revolutionary governments threaten U.S. security should be looked at with a sense of proportion and a degree of common sense. Clearly, an offensive Soviet deployment in the Western hemisphere—in Nicaragua for instance—would be a dangerous escalation in an arms race that is already out of control. Even now, however, Soviet submarines are poised off U.S. shores with nuclear weapons able to reach their targets in minutes. Moreover, for a tiny

Central American country to accept Soviet missles would be suicidal, since it would immediately become a nuclear target.

The argument that Soviet-linked revolutionary regimes in Central America threaten vital U.S. sea lanes assumes a peculiar situation in which: (a) the United States is engaged militarily with the Soviet Union (b) in a confrontation that is both prolonged and non-nuclear and (c) in which the USSR and its Central American ally judge they can attack U.S. shipping without provoking an all-out attack against the ally or a dangerous escalation against the USSR.

In reality, any military confrontation between the United States and the USSR, even if it began with conventional weapons, would be almost certain either to escalate rapidly or to move toward negotiations. Again, it would be suicidal for a tiny Central American country to make itself a target for the United States.

Those whose main focus is U.S. security argue that a Central American country might allow the USSR to install naval facilities that would enhance its Caribbean presence, but it is hard to see what that would add to what the USSR has had in Cuba for two decades.

Despite its inherent irrationality, the possibility that a revolutionary country might provide the Soviet Union with some offensive military capability, in return for military protection, economic aid, or trade, cannot be utterly excluded. After all, that is what Cuba did in the early 1960s. Preventing such an outcome should be an ultimate consideration for the United States. Hence, one aim of a negotiated approach should be to remove Central American conflicts from the arena of East-West confrontation.

Some here in the United States assert that Marxist governments in Central America will generate hordes, perhaps millions, of "feet people," refugees fleeing totalitarianism, and that they will head for the United States. First it should be noted that already an estimated 300,000 Salvadorans and Guatemalans have come to the United States—fleeing not Marxism, but the violence of their own governments.

Some Nicaraguans fled the Sandinista revolution either with Somoza or later. Most of those who arrived in the United States are not properly refugees but expatriates—they chose to leave Nicaragua because they anticipated that their standard of living could decline under the revolution. Some poor Nicaraguans also fled, particularly Miskito Indians who escaped to Honduras. Should a revolutionary government come to power in El Salvador, no doubt some people will flee, either because they believe their standard of living will fall or because they fear the consequences of their ties to the army or government.

It is not the advent of revolutionary governments that is most likely to generate large numbers of refugees, however. Rather, it is an ever more protracted and destructive war that will uproot people from their land and destroy their country's economy. The resolution to the refugee problem would be an end to the wars. It is interesting to note that most refugees who fled the attacks of Somoza's National Guard in Nicaragua returned when the war ended.

The credibility argument—that is, that Central America is a test of U.S. resolve and power which has grave implications elsewhere— is dangerous and pernicious. Over the long run, neither of the superpowers can permanently impose its will on other nations. Security must be grounded not in military might but in respect for the rights of others, for self-determination, and for pluralism and diversity. American citizens should not be made to feel that their sense of self-worth depends on their government's ability to "prevail" in tiny countries almost a thousand miles from their border.

No one doubts that the United States is technologically capable of turning Central America into a smoking wasteland. What is really in question is whether it will have the wisdom to seek solutions that can end the causes of strife and rebellion. This sort of credibility has ramifications that go beyond Central America.

WHAT DO THE REVOLUTIONARIES WANT?

According to a prevalent stereotype, those who lead revolutions are power-hungry, ruthless, even bloodthirsty people, whose aim is to take over their countries in order to establish totalitarian regimes subordinate to the imperial aims of the Soviet Union. In that view, revolutions are irrational, a collective plunge into the abyss. They can be "understood" only as pathology.

The starting point here, on the contrary, is that Central American revolutions make sense—at least to those who have taken part in them. In many ways, revolutionaries themselves are as rational as corporation executives. They carefully calculate and weigh various options as they pursue their ends with single-minded determination. If their proposals and the means by which they would carry them out are better understood, then it will be much clearer to what extent their aims may be compatible with U.S. interests.

Assuming that Central American revolutionary movements embody proposals for meeting the aspirations of the population (whether they will work is a separate question), we shall examine the outlines of what these proposals entail on the basis of Sandinista government programs, documents of the Salvadoran and Guatemalan revolutionary movements, and analyses by Central American social scientists.

An End to Violence

Out of a concern to address the political and economic issues, the number one aspiration of people in Central America might be overlooked: peace. The basic reason for violence in Central America today is resistance to change on the part of those holding economic and political power. Many Central Americans have joined the guerrillas out of what they see as a need for self-defense: for them the army is the aggressor.

Not only must the murders and massacres be ended, but people must feel that their lives are secure. Despite the undeniable military buildup in Nicaragua, most citizens see the Sandinista army and police not as a repressive force but as supportive of the revolution they are seeking to build. Their insecurity comes from the U.S.-backed *contras*. A first aspiration is peace and security.

A New Economic Model

All observers recognize that any solution in Central America must entail economic change. What the United States has proposed, however, is largely an infusion of aid in massive amounts. To the extent that there is any notion of a new approach to development, it is that Central America and Caribbean countries should encourage export industries, such as those in Puerto Rico or Taiwan. As in those countries, corporations would be attracted by the comparative advantage of cheap labor. However, because they are so keyed to the export market, such industries are not too dissimilar to the banana plantations of old. They do little for genuine internal development. Moreover, the world economy has room for only a few Taiwans and Puerto Ricos, and Central America's present instability will make outside investors wary for quite some time.

Over the last twenty years, Latin American economists and social scientists have developed a critique of existing models of development. This whole body of sometimes conflicting theories (dependence, world-systems, modes of production) is essentially negative. It explains why development is not working for the bulk of the population, but says little about what should be done. Since no Latin American country has undertaken serious structural reform between the 1973 coup in Chile and the Nicaraguan revolution, this is hardly surprising.

With the advent of the Nicaraguan revolution, social scientists from Central America and the Caribbean countries have been stimulated to seek an alternative model of development, one that would begin to meet the basic needs of the population—in their words, one where the economy would follow the "logic of the majorities." Like many Latin American intellectuals, these scholars are sympathetic to Marxism. Nevertheless, they have had to recognize that classical Marxist theory offers relatively little help for the real situations in their countries. Both Russia and China, the two classical cases of attempted transition to socialism, have huge populations and vast natural resources. They were able to turn inward and attempt sweeping experiments within their own borders. Whatever one may think of the results, they have little to say to the tiny nations of Central America and the Caribbean. Hence, these social scientists began by analyzing the peculiar features of their region and their countries.

All these countries have small open agroexport economies. They do not produce capital goods and will not be able to do so, given their size. Machinery for industrialization can become available only with foreign exchange earned through agroexports. Their real interests will best be served if they can remain part of the Western economic system in order to have both the widest markets for their products and access to Western machinery and technology.

An adequate development strategy must first seek to meet the basic needs of the population. Yet it must also lay the groundwork for rational industrialization by finding a new model of saving and of investment in capital goods for further development.

Food self-sufficiency must be part of the starting point. In recent decades, the landholding elites have expanded agroexports at the expense of the production of basic foods such as corn and beans. Nicaragua has made strides toward self-sufficiency in basic foods, but it is also finding that increasing the real income of the poor increases demand even for those basic food items.

Basic grains like corn and beans are produced by individual peasants working small tracts of land. While a doctrinaire application of Marxist theory might point toward collectivization, the experience of socialist countries shows that this does not lead to efficient agriculture. Moreover, Central American peasants expect not grandiose schemes but control over the land they work and fair prices for what they produce, although they are quite willing to work together and to try new techniques and new methods of organization.

Similarly, an industrialization strategy should emphasize the production of articles for the daily use of the majority instead of luxury items that only a few people can afford—for example, affordable soap instead of expensive scented varieties with foreign brand names. At present, much manufacturing takes place in small artisan shops. It might make sense to stimulate this artisan production and integrate it into overall national plans.

Until now, most of the profits from the mainspring of their economy, agroexports, have gone to foreign investors or to national oligarchies for their own luxury consumption or into their foreign bank accounts; only to some extent have profits been reinvested in the countries themselves. In the 1960s the agroexport class used its profits to become partners of the multinationals that were attracted to the Central American Common Market. A new economic model must center on a new kind of accumulation—that is, on generating savings for investment in solid development that will benefit the majority of the population. With this in mind, Nicaragua, even while it has sought to become self-sufficient in basic food production, is also expanding and modernizing agroexport production—for instance, it is building new sugar mills to bring in needed foreign exchange.

Until now, each of the small countries of the Carribbean and Central America has related bilaterally to its trading partners in North America and Europe. They have competed with each other in marketing the same tropical products. A key component in a new development strategy would make their economies more complementary and increase intraregional trade. (A political corollary is that diverse kinds of governments should find ways of working together toward common development aims.)

All of this implies a strong state role in the economy, especially in controlling strategic sectors such as banking, finance, and foreign trade. It does not necessarily entail a state-owned economy. The decisive question is not ownership but rather the thrust of the economy and whose interests are served. When a relatively small group—an oligarchy—effectively controls a country's economy by means of its institutions and its veto power over the government, it can determine what is produced and for whom.

A concept from conventional economics will illustrate the point. Economists speak of "consumer sovereignty," meaning that people "vote" when they spend their money, buying one brand instead of another, or simply choosing from among countless other ways to use their money. However, if 2 percent of the population receives twice as much income as the whole bottom half of the population, it can easily "outvote" the majority—for instance, by importing Mercedes-Benz automobiles—while the bulk of the population scarcely has the economic votes to demand subsistence rations of corn and beans. Strong state support of the efforts of the poor to organize can begin to rectify this imbalance and move toward greater equity.

The Sandinistas and other Central American revolutionaries say they intend to maintain a "mixed economy"—that is, one made up of private, state, and cooperative sectors. Some might see here a tactical ploy to allay fears and to hide an intention of eventually instituting an entirely state-owned and -run economy. However, it should be noted that what is frequently regarded as the private sector—that is, the larger plantations and businesses—is only part of the story. The whole private sector extends from small peasant tracts and village stores through medium-sized enterprises to large private operations. In Nicaragua, small and medium-sized enterprises do not feel threatened by the revolution. It is only the owners of larger enterprises (actually quite modest by U.S. standards) who feel that the revolution is unfair—primarily because their profits are now limited and they no longer set the rules. Some businesses do decline in a revolution, primarily luxury imports. On the other hand, some owners of large plantations worth millions of dollars have quietly continued to produce within the context of the revolution.

One other observation may help put the question of the state's role in the economy into perspective. Even if the Nicaraguan government were to take possession of the country's entire economy, its total gross national product of $2.4 billion in 1982 would put it far below the fiftieth largest industrial corporation in the United States—Monsanto, whose sales totaled $6.9 billion. It would even stand slightly below McDonald's, whose sales reached $2.5 billion. In a world economy dominated by giant multinational corporations, it is only logical that Third World countries would want to acquire some muscle through strong state participation in the economy. In both capitalist Mexico and Brazil, state enterprises are major economic actors.

In sum, based on a growing body of research and analysis, Central American revolutionaries hope to foment a new kind of mixed economy with strong state participation that will reorient production toward meeting basic needs (especially food self-sufficiency) and at the same time lay the groundwork for further integrated development.

Political Participation

Strictly speaking, the political systems of sovereign countries are internal matters—except where gross violations of human rights become a concern of the international community. Thus, in principle, which political forms a revolutionary government adopts should not be of direct concern to U.S. policy. Nevertheless, since much of the debate in Central America pits "democratic" El Salvador and Honduras against "totalitarian" Nicaragua, some discussion of the political aims of revolutionary groups is necessary.

The carrying out of revolutionary change requires power and an effective revolutionary party and state. It also demands the active participation of the population. In fact, it is in this active participation in changing social and economic structures and building a new kind of society that revolutionaries see as the essence of democracy. For them, politics is a matter of ongoing popular involvement. A prime example of this is Nicargua's 1980 literacy crusade. At that time some 60,000 students left their classrooms and went into the countryside for five months to teach peasants to read and write, while some 35,000 more taught in their own areas. Some 500,000 peasants learned to read and write, thus lowering the illiteracy rate from 52 percent to 13 percent. At the same time, the students came face-to-face with the real Nicaragua by living in peasant huts, sharing simple food, and sometimes going hungry.

Seen from this angle, it is electoral politics that appears undemocratic. If the central political act is voting periodically for candidates preselected by parties controlled by dominant elites, then democracy is not served. Although, in principle, voting allows people to "throw the rascals out" in such countries as El Salvador, the real rascals in the military and oligarchy are beyond the reach of the electoral process. Institutions such as political parties and congresses primarily provide an arena in which elites can struggle over secondary issues and seemingly legitimize the overall power arrangements in society.

This is not to argue that the revolutionary concept is superior. Certainly, the historical record of "people's democracies" reveals a great deal of hypocrisy, deceit, and crime. Within them, the most critical issues, especially regarding foreign policy, are argued only in closed party chambers. Without genuine public opposition, revolutionary parties can cease to be accountable to the people whom they ostensibly serve.

On the other hand, shopfloor democracy seems to function in some socialist countries. In Yugoslavia, for example, both factory and office workers have an integral role in management decisions.

The point here is modest. While the aspiration for democracy is broad, no particular form is finished or perfect. Indeed, democracy is unfinished business around the world. We might recall that one of the demands of the Solidarity Movement in Poland was that workers be involved in the hiring and firing of supervisors. Such a demand would seem utterly alien to most Americans, and yet people in Solidarity saw it as a logical democratic aspiration.

By the same token, revolutionary political forms may make sense to people in revolutionary countries. The crucial question for U.S. policy should be not whether such forms are congruent with U.S. notions of democracy, but whether they enjoy sufficient legitimacy from their own people.

Nonalignment

The Sandinistas and the revolutionary opposition movements in El Salvador and Guatemala see themselves as part of the Third World and would describe their approach to foreign policy as "nonalignment." However, both the U.S. government and the U.S. public find it difficult to accept nonalignment. The feeling that those who are not completely with us are against us runs deep, and the low esteem (and even contempt) shown for the United Nations in the United

States seems to reflect a feeling that it is primarily a forum for up-start nations to berate this country.

This difficulty is compounded when former client states assert their independence. Some might see Nicaragua as following a Soviet line in international forums. In fact, such votes are actually follow-ing a world-wide pattern. All Third World countries tend to vote against the United States to a greater or lesser extent. Of all votes cast in the Thirty-Eighth General Assembly of the United Nations, the average rate of agreement with the United States for all Third World countries was 18.9 percent—while Nicaragua voted with the United States 14.1 percent of the time.

In seeking a modus vivendi in Central America, the United States would have to acknowledge the right to genuine nonalignment, in-cluding the right to maintain trade and diplomatic relations with socialist countries.

ACCOMMODATION WITH THE UNITED STATES

This discussion has tried to make a reasonable case. To what extent, however, can one assume that revolutionaries are reasonable? Upon taking power, will they not show their true colors—say, by forcing out the civilian politicians whom they have used to front for them? First, it should be recalled that the opposition movements are broad and diverse. Moreover, engaging in guerrilla warfare for years is not a preparation for organizing an economy, carrying out land reform, managing state enterprises, reorganizing health care, increasing lit-eracy, reforming educational systems and curricula, dealing with other governments, or negotiating with banks and multinational cor-porations. All these tasks demand large numbers of qualified people. Most will not be Marxists, even if they agree with the overall aims of the revolution and employ some Marxist terminology.

To take an example from Nicaragua, successive economic plans have been the product of a continued and intense discussion between government technocrats and Sandinista leaders, taking into account complex issues such as whether the agricultural wage should be raised (with the consequent risk of inflation) and what to do about the enormous inherited foreign debt. Many of these technocrats were managers in the private sector before the revolution. These discussions have amounted to an ongoing course in economics and business management for people who have spent their previous years in the mountains. Some "moderates" who have left the government, like Arturo Cruz, former ambassador to the United States, have received considerable media attention; what goes unnoticed is that many moderates have been working in the Sandinista government for five years and continue to do so. Indeed, the Sandinista government sends administrators to a training institution in Managua run by the Harvard Business School.

Just as revolutionary movements acknowledge their need for civilian expertise and broad-based coalitions to carry out the reforms they envision, they are pragmatic enough to recognize that they are located in what the United States has long regarded as its backyard. Their economies are tied to those of the West. The United States has been the largest market for the region's agroexports and the primary source of its imports. In many cases, it would be too costly to switch to other kinds of equipment or technology. Even if they should desire to diversify their economic relations, it would be in their interest to remain within the Western economic system.

Moreover, the Soviet Union is clearly not willing to offer Nicaragua or any other Central American nation the large amounts of aid it would need to break away from the Western economic system. The Soviet Union may strain to support Cuba, but there is little reason to believe it could adopt other such clients. Because they would want to remain nonaligned, Central American revolutionary governments would no doubt establish relations with the Eastern bloc, but they could expect no more than modest aid.

Finally, it would in no sense be in their interest for Central American revolutionary governments to face the active hostility of the United States. The resources employed against the Sandinistas are a negligible part of the U.S. budget, and yet they force the Nicaraguan government and people to bring major development efforts to a standstill and to shift to a defense-and-survival economy.

To conclude the point: Central American revolutionary movements, should they take power, would have every reason to reach an accommodation with the United States.

There is no inherent reason why the United States could not reach an accommodation with revolutionary movements in Central America. To do so, of course, the United States would have to distinguish between its own long-range interests as a whole and the interests of particular parties who fear the consequences of any revolution. It would have to recognize that it is dealing with small agroexport countries that pose no genuine security threat to the hemisphere, and it would have to be sophisticated enough to take a pragmatic (rather than an ideological) approach to relations with these countries.

A final objection should be considered. Some might believe that an accommodation with revolutionary movements in Central America would encourage revolutionary movements in other Latin American countries where U.S. interests are much greater (such as Mexico, Brazil, and Chile). Although it is never stated, this fear may be the real bottom line in economic terms. The United States' investment in Central America is only a minuscule 2.5 percent of its total investment in Latin America. But just as the Chilean coup was a devastating reminder to many Latin Americans that basic change may take many years, even generations, the Nicaraguan revolution has energized many with a sense of hope. Its demonstration effect is real.

However, it is ethically repugnant to think that Central Americans should have to continue to die in large numbers simply to send a message about U.S. determination. Central America belongs to Central Americans—properly speaking, the United States cannot lose it at all. Revolutions can come only from within a people. An outside demonstration effect can at most help people overcome psychological barriers and enable them to believe that victory is possible, but it will not supply any of the basic conditions for revolution. If U.S. policymakers or local elites are concerned about further revolutions, the lesson of Central America should impel them to examine whether similar structural conditions exist elsewhere and whether people's basic aspirations are being frustrated in a similar manner.

SIX

WHAT TO DO

Inherent in the premises of present U.S. policy in Central America is a thrust toward direct involvement in combat and a widening war. That is why other governments, Central America experts, churches, citizens' groups, and congressional representatives have all urged negotiations as an alternative. Such an insistent clamor has obliged the Reagan administration to adopt at least the rhetoric of negotiation.

This final chapter analyzes the issues involved in a negotiated approach and sketches what such an approach would entail for U.S. policy.

NEGOTIATION REJECTED

Even in 1980 there were proposals for negotiated alternatives in Central America. Since that time, there have been numerous appeals in that direction and several specific proposals made by heads of state, political parties, and church officials (see Chronology, pp. 129–135). Individual scholars and commissions such as the prestigious Inter-American Dialogue, headed by former U.S. Ambassador Sol Linowitz and Galo Plaza, ex-president of Ecuador, have urged a negotiated approach regarding both Nicaragua and El Salvador.

Such appeals and proposals have been consistently ignored or thwarted by the United States. Two presidents of Mexico, José López Portillo and Miguel de la Madrid Hurtado, have made proposals and sought to warn the Reagan administration and the U.S. public of the dangers of this country's present militaristic approach. Yet, as a memorandum from a National Security Council meeting of April 1982 indicates, the Reagan administration has regarded Mexico's efforts not as a resource to be used, but as a problem to be managed. Similarly, the efforts of President Herrera Campins of Venezuela, General Torrijos of Panama, and President Monge of Costa Rica have been frustrated.

A most revealing example occurred in 1981 when Archbishop Arturo Rivera y Damas of San Salvador, who had made every effort to be even-handed since replacing Archbishop Romero, carefully sought to create conditions for negotiations. He first checked with the FDR and Duarte, then went to Europe to consult with Social Democratic and Christian Democratic parties, and to report to the pope. Upon his arrival in Washington, however, Deputy Secretary of State William Clark and Vice-President Bush refused his offer. This, it should be recalled, was shortly after the FMLN's first offensive, which U.S. spokespersons confidently called a failure.

The United States has engaged in diplomacy of its own, but its overall effect has been to thwart genuine negotiated solutions. In 1981, Assistant Secretary of State for Latin America Thomas Enders went to Managua, seemingly to propose grounds for a U.S. accommodation with Nicaragua. However, his message was essentially an ultimatum that unless Nicaragua behaved as the United States wanted, it would have to face active U.S. hostility. In April 1982, U.S. proposals also made the cessation of Nicaraguan arms shipments to El Salvador (for which it could offer no proof) the condition for even beginning negotiations. In 1982 the presidents of Mexico and Venezuela feared that cross-border raids on Nicaragua from Honduras would develop into a border war, and they therefore offered their services as mediators. The Honduran president, Roberto Suazo Córdoba, accepted the offer but the United States countered by organizing a "Peace Forum" in Costa Rica, taking advantage of that country's democratic image. Mexico and Venezuela did not attend. Similarly, in 1984, after more than a year of preparatory work, the Contadora Group put forward a series of peace treaties. When Nicaragua declared its willingness to accept the treaties, the United States expressed its displeasure; and shortly thereafter its allies, El Salvador, Costa Rica, and Honduras, were also finding the treaties unacceptable—even though they had been consulted extensively during the drafting work.

Formal statements notwithstanding, for over four years the United States has consistently refused to seriously undertake negotiated approaches in Central America.

The United States seems prepared to use diplomacy only if it will achieve what could be achieved by force. That is, the United States is prepared to negotiate only the surrender of the FMLN in El Salvador and the capitulation of the Sandinista government to U.S. hegemony.

The Kissinger Commission report provides a revealing example of this underlying mentality. After proposing vast increases in military aid, Chapter 6 ("Central America Security Issues") ends with a short paragraph transitional to the final chapter, which deals with diplomacy.

> We would hope, moreover, that a clear U.S. commitment to such a course would itself improve the prospects for successful negotiations—so that *arms would support diplomacy rather than supplant it.* [Emphasis added.]

Obviously arms "support" diplomacy precisely by being ready to "supplant" it.

Diplomacy is seen as preferable to direct intervention, but what remains invariable is the United States' determination to direct the outcome. After listing some "underpinnings" for a "successful political strategy" the report's opening discussion of diplomacy states:

> At the same time, there is little doubt that the projection of U.S. power, in some form, will be required to preserve the interests of the United States and of other nations in the region. A nation can project power without employing its forces in military encounter. However, a basic rule of statescraft is that assessment of risks is the solvent of diplomacy. In this case, *we can expect negotiations to succeed only if those we seek to persuade have a clear understanding that there are circumstances in which the use of force, by the United States or by others, could become necessary as a last resort.* [Emphasis added.]

Lest there be any doubt over who needs to be "persuaded," the Commission says specifically:

> Finally, as part of the backdrop to diplomacy, Nicaragua must be aware that force remains an ultimate recourse. The United States and the countries of the region retain this option.

That option, the commission adds, should be only a "course of last resort and only where there are clear dangers to U.S. security." Diplomacy seems to be regarded as a continuation of war by other means.

The report's graduate seminar tone may obscure the elementary fact that the world's most powerful country is threatening to unleash its military machine against the tiny, weak nations of Central America. All negotiations require compromises and concessions. Perhaps the key "concession" the United States will have to make is to acknowledge that it is dealing with sovereign nations on whom it can no longer impose its will, even in what some still regard as its backyard.

THE CONTADORA INITIATIVE

If any countries could claim that Central America was in their backyard, it would be those adjacent: Mexico, Panama, Colombia, and Venezuela—the so-called Contadora group. Yet it is these nations that have made sustained efforts to find negotiated solutions since early 1983.

None of these governments are left-wing: they have become involved for pragmatic, not ideological, reasons. Instability threatens them, and they recognize that all parties will lose in the regional war entailed in U.S. policies that treat Central America solely as an arena of East-West confrontation in which the West must prevail.

Their Latin American identity may be another motivating factor for the Contadora governments. Latin Americans of all stripes, from leftists to conservatives, bear a memory of U.S. heavy-handedness in their region. They view the Monroe Doctrine, for example, not as an altruistic offer of protection against outside aggression but as a unilateral U.S. declaration of a right to intervene.

In this light, we may view Contadora as an assertion by Latin American governments that they are mature and capable of carrying out a diplomacy that might save the United States from the disastrous consequences inherent in its present policies. Latin Americans feel they are able to understand the crisis in Central America. They insist that the conflicts are primarily internal and should not be defined as problems of East-West confrontation. Brazil, Argentina, Bolivia, and Ecuador have expressed their support for the Contadora initiatives, as have Canada and most European governments.

Procedurally, the Contadora Group began by seeking to mediate border disputes, especially those between Honduras and Nicaragua, and thereby reduce the danger of war. The group has since sought to move from general principles, subscribed to by the five Central American countries, toward verifiable and binding treaties.

In September 1983, the Contadora countries drew up Twenty-One Points, principles that could provide a basis for settling conflicts. Aside from those dealing with trade, aid, and development, and others on "democratization" (the result of lobbying by El Salvador, Costa Rica, and Honduras to draw attention to the fact that Nicaragua had not held elections), the main planks expressed the intentions of the region's governments to:

- Halt the arms race in all its manifestations and initiate negotiations on the subject of control and reduction of the current arms inventory and actual number of arms.
- Forbid the establishment in the region of foreign military bases or any other form of foreign military interference.
- Concert agreements to reduce, and eventually eliminate, the presence of foreign military advisers and other forms of foreign military and security actions.
- Establish international mechanisms of control for the prevention of the traffic of arms from the territory of one country to the region of another.
- Eliminate the traffic of arms, within the region or from abroad, forwarded to persons, organizations, or groups attempting to undermine Central American governments.
- Prevent the use of their own territory for, and neither to lend nor allow, military or logistic support to persons, organizations, or groups attempting to destabilize Central American governments.
- Abstain from promoting or supporting acts of terrorism, subversion, or sabotage in the countries of the area.
- Create mechanisms and coordinate systems of direct communication aimed to prevent or, if necessary, to resolve incidents among states of the region.

These were simply guidelines that the Contadora Group intended to translate into verifiable and binding treaties.

Such principles, if accepted and adhered to, would satisfy U.S. requirements regarding its own security. Soviet or Cuban military bases would be excluded, military advisors and other forms of foreign presence in Nicaragua would be reduced and then eliminated, and any arms traffic from the Sandinistas to the Salvadoran insurgents would be ended.

However, the Contadora principles would apply equally to U.S. bases in Honduras, U.S. advisors and military aid to El Salvador, and the U.S. support for the *contras*. It is because of the requirements of this reciprocity that the United States has consistently refused to support the Contadora process, and has largely thwarted it.

Applied across the board, the Contadora proposals would frustrate U.S. policy objectives. If the *contras* were deprived of their sanctuaries in Costa Rica and Honduras, their supplies from the U.S. and Honduran armies, and their CIA funding, they would cease to be a serious threat to the Sandinista government. The Salvadoran insurgency's main strength, on the other hand, is internal. It is the government and army that are propped up by the United States. Even a curtailing of U.S. aid and hints that the army might not be able to count on the United States as its ultimate backup might induce panic—or force the Salvadoran government to agree to negotiations.

In this light, it is not surprising that despite its verbal support, the Reagan administration has in fact undermined the Contadora process. During the first half of 1983, it largely ignored the group's initial diplomatic efforts. In July, whether by design or by coincidence, at the very moment that the Contadora countries were making proposals and the Sandinistas were for the first time accepting the principle of multilateral negotiations, President Reagan sent U.S. warships to patrol both coasts of Nicaragua and announced extensive U.S. military maneuvers in Honduras—actions that were taken as direct threats by the Sandinistas. In September 1983, as the five Central American governments were accepting the Twenty-One Points, the United States was reconstituting the Central American Defense Council (CONDECA) with Honduras, El Salvador, and Guatemala as members. The result was the creation of a potential regional army that could attack Nicaragua or fight the Salvadoran insurgents.

Despite the Reagan administration's efforts to thwart the Contadora effort, the negotiating teams patiently worked to put the Twenty-One Points into treaty form. At one point, over one hundred technical advisors and diplomats were involved. Finally on September 7, 1984, the four Contadora countries agreed on a compromise version and submitted it to the Central American governments, which had been consulted extensively during its preparation.

If implemented, the proposed treaty would reverse the present thrust toward militarization in several ways. The countries of the region would agree to submit inventories of their present arms, suspend new arms acquisitions, and establish limits on certain types of equipment, particularly offensive weapons. Next they would establish limits on personnel. A Commission of Verification and Control, made up of four other Latin American countries, would assure compliance. Moreover, the governments would agree to not authorize foreign military bases, and to eliminate existing ones within six months of signing the treaty. International military maneuvers would be forbidden. Other provisions dealt with foreign military advisors, and with support for insurgencies or terrorism in other countries. Following recommendations by the United States and its allies, there were also provisions on electoral processes.

Nicaragua agreed to the draft version on September 21. Although it had frequently voiced its verbal support, the Reagan administration was caught off guard. Administration spokespersons called the treaty proposals unfair, citing for example the fact that foreign military advisors engaged in training and operations (such as U.S. personnel in El Salvador) would have to leave while those involved in maintenance (such as the Cubans and Soviets in Nicaragua) would not. They further stated that it was one-sided to end U.S. military exercises and close U.S. military bases without exacting anything from Nicaragua. However, that objection only underscores the one-sidedness of U.S. military involvement: no other foreign power was constructing bases or holding maneuvers. The Reagan administration also feared that Nicaragua would be allowed to retain large military forces. Stated another way, this was simply a recognition that a neutral commission might well accept Nicaragua's argument that it needed a large military force to deter a U.S. invasion.

By October 19 the U.S. allies, Honduras, El Salvador, and Costa Rica, had come back with a counterproposal, eliminating or attenuating some of the Contadora proposals and adding the Central American nations themselves to the verification commission. That proposal would make it much less likely that the commission itself could be truly neutral, especially regarding Nicaragua.

Neither Mexico nor Venezuela regarded the September 7 treaty as unfair. It remained to be seen whether Contadora had been destroyed, or whether it could yet prove to be a vehicle for a diplomatic solution.

The U.S. rejection of the Contadora initiatives reflects a characteristic American attitude that goes beyond the Reagan administration. The United States objects to foreign intervention in Central America but seems blind to the fact that in Central America the United States itself is a "foreign" power—arguably more so than Cuba. This blind spot is especially obvious in the Kissinger Commission report.

U.S. intervention in Central America not only is foreign but is on a scale far exceeding that of any other foreign actor. In both 1983 and 1984, U.S. expenditures in the region exceeded $700 million, not including the cost of extensive military maneuvers, which came from the Pentagon budget and cost many more millions.

President Miguel de la Madrid of Mexico presented many of these themes in an address to the U.S. Congress in May 1984. He stressed that Central America should not become a theater for East-West confrontation and reforms should not be regarded as threatening security: "We therefore reject, without exception, all military plans that would seriously endanger the security and development of the region. . . . For our countries, it is obvious that reason and understanding are superior to the illusion of the effectiveness of force."

NEGOTIATED SETTLEMENTS

In themselves, the countries of Central America are not of vital concern to U.S. interests—they have few important natural resources, and only a minute share of direct U.S. investment in Latin America is located there. Therefore, U.S. aims in seeking solutions to the crisis may be expressed in minimal terms: that there be no threat to U.S. security and that there be stability in the region (see Chapter 5).

However, a genuine solution must take into account the background of the crisis and must create conditions in which the peoples of the region themselves enjoy enough security to confront their own development problems. These include both the immediate problems occasioned by the world recession, such as their debt, and the long-range problems rooted in structural conditions.

Some might harbor a notion that the United States itself could undertake a Camp David–type peacemaking role—such is the impression reinforced by President Reagan's appointment of a roving envoy in the region. As the Salvadoran insurgents pointed out, however, since that envoy represented one of the parties in conflict, he was in no way neutral. (As if to corroborate this point, Ambassador Richard Stone devoted some of his negotiating time to the problem of unifying the feuding Nicaraguan *contras*.)

The Contadora countries, or a similar group, would have to undertake the mediation role. That these countries are staunch U.S. allies and not leftist should furnish some reassurance.

Some have held that a negotiated settlement should be a single regional package; they argue that there is a symmetry between the conflicts in Nicaragua and El Salvador. In each case a government is threatened by an insurgency that has connections to other governments. The implication—not spelled out—is that a settlement might involve tradeoffs—for instance, a left-reform government in El Salvador in return for a more "moderate" government in Nicaragua.

This notion has only superficial plausibility. In reality, the Nicaraguan revolutionary government is seeking to address the real needs of the majority of the people and because of that has a basic legitimacy and widespread popular support. It was the CIA, not pervasive internal discontent, that turned the *contras* into an army. They are utterly dependent on their U.S. backing. By contrast, the Salvadoran government and military have made themselves illegitimate by their involvement in the murder of close to 1 percent of the citizenry. They face a revolution that enjoys considerable legitimacy and is the outgrowth of ten or fifteen years of grassroots struggle. The situations are not comparable and formal symmetry provides no genuine basis for a negotiated approach. Nevertheless, a comprehensive regional approach may be desirable.

Genuine negotiations involve compromise and concessions. If there is to be peace in Central America, all sides will have to accept something less than what they would regard as an optimal solution. The Sandinista government would find its natural desire to support revolutionary movements curtailed. Salvadoran insurgents might find themselves accepting a coalition government. The most repressive forces in Central America might find themselves out of the picture completely. For its part the United States would have to focus on safeguarding its fundamental interests and acknowledge that it can no longer dictate events in the region.

It is important to consider the issues for negotiation in particular countries.

Nicaragua

Issues the United States has raised for negotiation with Nicaragua can be summarized under four headings: (1) relations with Cuba and the Soviet Union, (2) a military buildup said to threaten its neighbors, (3) support for insurgency elsewhere in the region, and (4) the internal political framework.

We have already argued that it would be suicidal for Nicaragua or any country to accept Soviet deployment of an offensive military installation, insofar as that country would thereby become a target (probably nuclear) of the United States.

What could make Nicaragua even consider such deployment, and certainly what impels its military buildup, is a possible direct U.S. attack aimed at overthrowing the revolution. That buildup, however, understandably disturbs Honduras and Costa Rica—or at least their elites. But it is unrealistic to expect Nicaragua to reduce its armed forces until it is assured that it will not be attacked by the United States.

Nicaragua must come to be convinced that the United States will not attack it—that the United States is reconciled to the existence of a revolutionary state on the mainland of the Western hemisphere. Obviously, the Sandinistas will want more than verbal assurances.

To this end, the United States should cease funding the *contras* and, in effect, disband them. If they obtain private funding, the United States should make it clear that it will not aid them; and Honduras and Costa Rica, following the Contadora conditions, must refuse to harbor them. Some might feel that the United States would thus be sacrificing a bargaining chip without gaining anything in return, but in fact, ending U.S. sponsorship for the *contras* must be a starting point. (The United States, however, would have a responsibility to aid individual *contras* either to accept an amnesty offer from Nicaragua or to resettle elsewhere.)

Nicaragua and its neighbors, Honduras and Costa Rica, could find ways of reducing tensions and possible conflicts. (Note that Honduras and Costa Rica apparently accepted the September 1984 Contadora treaty proposals until the United States reacted to Nicaragua's acceptance.) All sides could take an arms inventory; Nicaragua could agree to reduce its weapons and lower the number of soldiers and militia members according to an agreed-upon schedule, beginning with offensive weapons (for example, keeping its anti-aircraft batteries but reducing its number of tanks).

The Sandinistas have made no secret of their moral support for the Salvadoran revolution. Ordinary Nicaraguans identify with the struggles in El Salvador and Guatemala, recalling their own struggle against Somoza, in which over 2 percent of the population was killed. However, except for the brief period from late 1980 to early 1981, there is little indication of substantial arms shipments to the Salvadoran guerrillas. Salvadoran revolutionary groups have offices in Managua and no doubt have significant contact with the Sandinistas, but there is no evidence that their command-and-control center is in Managua. The United States accuses the Sandinistas of sponsoring terrorist activities in Costa Rica and Honduras. It is, of course, possible that some Sandinistas have had contact with incipient revolutionary movements in those countries, but that in itself does not constitute support for terrorism.

In any case, if implemented, the Contadora principles would prohibit arms shipments or other logistical support and aid to revolutionary groups in other countries. Presumably they would not exclude some expression of political solidarity with opposition groups. For example, the FMLN-FDR might continue to maintain offices and make international contacts in Nicaragua (as they do in Mexico and elsewhere). Yet if negotiations in El Salvador were underway, there would be no point in exporting revolution from Nicaragua. The Contadora principles would still apply to external support for Guatemalan insurgents, however.

The internal political arrangements of Nicaragua should not be a central topic for negotiations. Nevertheless, we may make some observations about how those arrangements might relate to U.S. policy.

The Sandinistas' basic legitimacy comes not from elections but from the anti-Somoza struggle and the ensuing efforts to carry out revolutionary change. As we have insisted, most Nicaraguans support—or at least accept—the Sandinista revolution, although a relatively small group is vehemently opposed because of the revolution's impact on their standard of living, power, and prestige.

Outside of this group, even those who are less than enthusiastic about the Sandinistas do not want to see them replaced by a "two-party system" that would simply mask real control by wealthy elites.

Unless the Sandinistas are overthrown militarily by the United States, they will remain the predominant political force in Nicaragua. Other political parties that endorse the overall goal of the revolution may have a role, perhaps an important and critical role, but they will not replace the Sandinistas. One-party rule is not necessarily totalitarian. Mexico, for example, has been under the de facto rule of one party for over fifty years. Yet the Mexican government, despite its corruption, is nevertheless more responsive to ordinary people than many other governments that are more formally "pluralistic."

It should not be assumed that if Nicaragua were more democratic it would be more "moderate." The Sandinistas may be restraining their own peasant and working-class followers as much as the business and upper-class groups. A more democratic process might enable peasants to pressure for the expropriation of large estates, or workers to pressure for lower salary differentials. Interestingly, if the Sandinistas were more "democratic" the results might be even more radical.

Only if they feel secure from outside threats will the Sandinistas feel free enough to experiment with wider democratic openings.

El Salvador

As this book has sought to make clear, the conflict in El Salvador is essentially an internal one and requires a solution that takes into account the process that produced it.

In advocating a "political settlement," the United States has repeatedly called for elections in which all parties, including the insurgent organizations, would participate. Conceding that the left might have legitimate fears, it has proposed that one element for negotiations would be its security. Any other proposals the United States has labeled as unacceptable "power-sharing" that would amount to allowing the left to "shoot its way into power."

Rather than rehashing the elections vs. power-sharing debate, let us examine the problems any political settlement must resolve.

Violence is the key issue, but it embraces far more than the issue of candidate safety. Since 1980, approximately 50,000 civilians have been killed in El Salvador. Some have been picked up, interrogated, and murdered by uniformed forces or death squads, or by paramilitary groups closely connected to the army; some have been slaughtered in mass killings as part of military sweeps; some have been killed during the bombings of civilian targets. Far from being occasional "abuses" or "excesses," these violent acts have amounted to de facto government policy. They have been essential in maintaining control over the population, in particular for keeping the opposition from organizing publicly in areas under government control. The Salvadoran government has persisted in resorting to such violence, despite the revulsion it has aroused in the U.S. public and Congress and the smoldering hatred it has generated among large sectors of El Salvador.

Any effective political solution would have to end this violence. It would not be enough simply to turn it off, so to speak, for the length of an electoral campaign. People could not reasonably be expected to shed their fear and act freely—even if the killing suddenly ceased for a period of months—as long as the individuals and institutions responsible for the violence were still in place. Those who dared to campaign actively on behalf of a leftist party, for example, would have to assume that intelligence services and unofficial informers were watching their every move. In fact, if the violence were simply turned off, intelligence services would no doubt take advantage of the respite to see which persons might reveal previously concealed political sympathies.

That is why the superficially attractive notion of an across-the-board amnesty would not work. There could be no effective political process as long as the capacity to resume killing civilians remained.

Indeed, the issue of violence affects not only the electoral period but the viability of the government that might result. Suppose, for example, that the violence did cease for a period of months and that out of a campaign period and election there emerged a coalition government made up of the left, reform groups, and a smaller group representing hard-line anticommunist sections. The elections would indicate a mandate for reforms. However, the newly elected reform government would probably be nullified by an unreformed army and still-existing death squads.

Consequently, it would seem that only if those responsible for the violence left the scene could there be a genuine political solution. One possibility might be to establish a clear legal proceeding for bringing to justice those responsible for atrocities during the war. Thus, criteria determining the definitions of atrocities, the kinds of evidence necessary, and the degree of responsibility constituting guilt (giving or carrying out orders, extenuating circumstances, and so on)' could be laid down. Judges and juries made up of respected people not identified with either side could be appointed. All sides would be liable to this proceeding: official forces, paramilitary groups, and guerrilla organizations. Finally, a grace period might allow individuals who feared being judged guilty time enough to leave the country. If, as human rights organizations and the Roman Catholic Church maintain, the official forces have been responsible for the vast majority of civilian deaths, it is probable that many soldiers and officers might seek exile. This could be an orderly way to "purge" the army and security forces and the guerrilla groups as well. Those remaining could be united into a new force with army and police functions.

We have left in brackets the question of what kind of authority would oversee such a process. Obviously it could not be the present military—nor could it be the civilian government, since it is utterly subordinate to the military. The need for something like the process we have described is no doubt what is behind proposals for a coalition government (what some call "power-sharing"). A transition government representing all sectors (including the FDR), and an armed forces (including the FMLN) would have the strength to deal with those responsible for the violence, especially if the United States made clear its support. Another formula might be a transition peacekeeping force made up of personnel from several Latin American countries.

With the problem of violence solved, at least in principle, a relatively simple political process could be set up. The essential aim would be to establish a procedure in which the Salvadoran people could express their will effectively. Clearly there is no unanimity in the population. Our assumption here is that in an open political process only a small percentage would vote for a hard-line, anti-left, anti-reform party like ARENA. How the vote might be divided is an open question. On the one hand, people might regard the Christian Democrats as partly responsible for the violence, insofar as their presence in the government has provided legitimacy for a policy of widespread murder. On the other hand, Christian Democrats themselves have been murdered by death squads, and a positive role in bringing about negotiations would win them popularity. It is possible that even some of the poor are apprehensive about Marxist movements. Since both the left and the reform elements agree in principle on broad issues such as land reform, they should be able to work together on common programs. Again, the challenge would be to work out a political process that would enable the Salvadoran people to express their real preferences, and for the resulting government to truly govern.

Clearly the sine qua non of such a process, whether it be guaranteed by a peacekeeping force or a coalition government, would be a political decision on the part of the United States to support the process and accept its results. (This would clearly constitute a major policy reversal, although it could no doubt be rationalized as representing what the United States had striven for all along.)

Economic reform should be an outgrowth of the political process—that is, of the will of the people as expressed in that process. However, it would be helpful if the broad outlines of economic reform were discussed in the negotiating process. For reasons discussed in Chapter 5, it should be possible to come to an agreement on a mixed economy with a state strong enough to lay down basic parameters and assure that priorities shift from elite private profits to meeting the basic needs of the poor. Many members of the oligarchy might very well elect to leave the country and live off their expatriated profits, but many smaller business and professional people could be encouraged to remain.

The FMLN-FDR position goes further than the one I am outlining here. As they see it, the violence is simply a symptom of the underlying problem, which is the effective power of the oligarchy over El Salvador. That power has not been broken, even by land reform. One sign has been the right wing's control of the assembly and specifically ARENA's control of the key economic ministries. As already noted (p. 73), in April 1984 the assembly blocked Phase II of the land reform (it had been suspended since the beginning) and halted Phase III, prompting the vice-minister of agriculture to say the land reform had been "formally paralyzed." Through the assembly, the oligarchy has successfully blocked increases of their own taxes and forced the cost of the war onto the bulk of the population by increasing direct taxes.

In the view of the FMLN-FDR, the elimination of the oligarchy's power is itself a necessary condition for a valid political solution to the country's problems, rather than part of a much longer-range transition process. By oligarchy they clearly do not mean the whole private sector, but those relatively few families that have the greatest proportion of the country's productive wealth, not only in land but also in industry and commerce.

If the oligarchy remained, with all its power, it could thwart any political settlement. The FMLN-FDR believes that a political solution must eliminate not only the symptom of violence, but its cause in the recalcitrance of the oligarchy.

A government emerging from a political settlement could have a nonaligned foreign policy. El Salvador would most probably identify with the Third World, keep its primary economic ties to the West, especially to Western Europe, and remain free to have economic, diplomatic, and cultural relations—but no significant military ties— with socialist countries.

The aim of the United States would be to keep the outcome as "moderate" as possible—that is, assure that the resulting government be truly nonaligned and that its economic changes be gradual.

The basic sequence for a political solution in El Salvador then would be as follows:

1. The United States would signal to the Salvadoran military and government its firm decision to seek a negotiated solution within the Contadora, or a similar, framework. It would in effect declare its intention to cease propping up the Salvadoran military and government. (Whether the termination would be gradual or abrupt would be a matter for prudential judgment.)
2. An outside force (such as Contadora) would oversee and facilitate the actual negotiations in which the Salvadoran government and military and the FMLN-FDR would be participants. The United States might participate formally, or through the Salvadoran government.
3. During the process of negotiations and elections, the government would be in the hands of a coalition group. Security functions would be carried out by an external peacekeeping force or by the combined forces of the present government and the FMLN-FDR (with those most responsible for the violence no longer present).
4. The central element would be to establish a political process,

including elections that could lead to a government that would represent the various sectors of the Salvadoran population, and such a process would have sufficient authority and power to govern and to initiate and carry out reforms.

Honduras and Costa Rica

A shift toward a negotiated approach would serve the real interests of both Honduras and Costa Rica, since they would be better able to address their own severe internal problems if they were no longer subordinated to U.S. strategic aims. They could enter into agreements with Nicaragua to reduce tensions by eliminating the cross-border movement of arms and insurgents.

There is no doubt Costa Ricans would prefer to concentrate on solving their own problems, and especially the financial crisis, while preserving their democratic traditions and avoiding the shift toward militarism.

In Honduras there is still a possibility that a coalition of reform-minded army officers and civilian politicians, with at least the acquiescence of business leaders, could work with peasant and labor organizations in fashioning a workable reform program.

Guatemala

As long as the Guatemalan army is the real arbiter, the United States should avoid any close relationship with that country. In such circumstances, even humanitarian and development aid serves to support the regime and is used as an element of counterinsurgency. U.S. policymakers should not be misled by elections and the facade of a civilian government. The army's policy of mass killings, forcible relocation, and massive forced organization of civilian militias has made the country a concentration camp.

While it is impossible to predict, one can hope that political settlements elsewhere in the region might have a positive effect on Guatemala.

Cuba

Since the Cuban government is at most a minor actor in Central America it would not be a party to the negotiations regarding Nicaragua and El Salvador. Regarding its relationship to Nicaragua or to any revolutionary movements, it could deal with the negotiating countries. It would not be a party, however, to matters in which it was not directly involved—for instance, the political process in El Salvador.

Cuba's participation should not depend on the state of its relations with the United States. Nevertheless, concurrent negotiations between Cuba and the United States could reinforce the process in Central America.

Reconstruction and Development

Chapter 2 has already argued that even large-scale economic aid such as that proposed by the Kissinger Commission would not address the underlying problems in Central America. Without peace and significant structural changes there can be no valid development.

If a peace along the lines advocated here were achieved, all the countries of Central America would still face enormous obstacles and would require external financial and development aid. The United States would have to decide to what extent it wished to be involved in such aid.

If negotiations led to the results outlined here—a consolidated Sandinista revolution in Nicaragua and a leftist-reform government in El Salvador—there might be considerable domestic opposition to any U.S. economic aid to such "unfriendly" countries. However, they might be able to receive significant aid from Western European governments. U.S. aid might be forthcoming to Costa Rica or Honduras, perhaps justified as necessary to prevent radicalization and revolution. By contributing to reconstruction and development aid, the United States could influence long-run outcomes.

Primacy should be given to those governments that make meeting the basic needs of their citizens the cornerstone of their economic policies. Both leftist Nicaragua and more moderate Costa Rica meet that criterion, as might a Salvadoran government that emerged from a genuine political settlement. It is possible that the ruling groups in Honduras might undertake genuine reform programs. However, unless the Guatemalan government made a clear commitment that it would use such aid for genuine development—a fundamental shift that is unforseeable at the moment—it should not receive significant funding. Where governments are unresponsive to the people's needs, private agencies may be valid channels for aid. They, at least, will reach people at the village level and may help them organize and work for change.

BEYOND CENTRAL AMERICA

Whatever the outcome in Central America, there will be further revolutions in Latin America and other parts of the world. There are signs in Peru, with its "Shining Light" revolutionaries; the Philippines, where the Marcos dictatorship seems to be re-enacting Somoza's script in a country twenty times larger; and South Africa, where even computer-age sophistication will be hard pressed to maintain apartheid over the people's basic aspiration for dignity. However, revolutions are essentially unpredictable, primarily because of the human factor—that is, people's courage, organizing ability, and persistence, as well as the errors of existing elites. If revolutions were predictable, well-funded think-tanks would have spotted the growing crisis in Central America long ago. Had they done so, the outcome might have been different.

New revolutions will not simply repeat the Central American experience. For example, large-scale nonviolent resistance may become more prominent in the future.

The important point here is that the way in which the United States deals with Central America will have long-term implications for foreign policy, probably in countries of much greater importance to the United States.

Currently it is out of fashion to speak of "North-South" issues, much less to use terms like interdependence or New International Economic Order. Despite the shift in the public mood, however, the reality remains: most of the world's human beings live in dire poverty while a small circle of nations, primarily those around the North Atlantic, dominate the world economy.

The problem of development is not yet solved. It is clear that Third World countries cannot simply repeat the stages of growth followed by the industrialized countries. There is really no model for small Third World countries to follow to both meet the needs of most of their people and achieve a kind of equitable growth and capital accumulation that will increase the living standards of all.

If peace were achieved, Central American countries could experiment with various approaches to development and might discover models that would answer some larger questions of global development. Similarly, developed nations, especially in Western Europe, might experiment with new forms of aid that could provide models for larger North-South issues.

Throughout, this book has argued that the trouble in Central America is not essentially the outgrowth of an East-West conflict. Nevertheless, successful negotiations in Central America might enhance the prestige of negotiation as an instrument of foreign policy. Conversely, if the United States cannot find an acceptable solution through negotiation in Central America, the prospects for a resolution of the much more complex and dangerous area of East-West confrontation would appear to be bleak.

Peace in Central America is a goal that appears frustratingly far away, especially when one hears the cries of the victims—the civilians abducted, tortured, and killed, or massacred in groups; the homeless and desperately hungry; those who have lost spouses, parents, children, and neighbors. United States policies have helped aggravate the conflicts and their causes. It is time to turn around and move toward peace, even if the path is uphill and the destination not yet clear.

Chronology of Central America Negotiations 1980–1984

Year	Month	Proposal	Response
1980		Archbishop Romero of *El Salvador* (murdered in March) calls for "dialogue."	
	Sept.	Salvadoran bishops offer to mediate.	FDR (Democratic Revolutionary Front) rejects offer, saying the bishops have no "moral authority" (i.e., they are linked to the repressive government).
	Nov.	"Dissent Memo," ostensibly by concerned U.S. government personnel, proposes a "Zimbabwe option" for *El Salvador* to the incoming Reagan administration. (The analogy is that the strongly ideological Thatcher was pragmatic in supporting a negotiated end to the civil war, even if the people elected a Marxist government.)	Memo ignored by Reagan administration.
1981	Jan.	As part of its "general offensive" the FDR-FMLN in *El Salvador* appoints a political-diplomatic commission that offers to negotiate but insists that negotiations include the United States as a party central to the conflict.	

Year	Month	Proposal	Response
1981	Jan.	The Socialist International makes repeated efforts to initiate negotiations between the Salvadoran government and the guerrillas in *El Salvador*.	
	Jan.	Panamanian General Torrijos (who has ongoing ties to the Salvadoran military) makes several efforts to initiate negotiations in *El Salvador*.	
	Jan.	Archbishop Rivera y Damas of *El Salvador* visits Washington to urge negotiations after having spoken with Duarte. He has the support of the pope, the FDR, and various European Social Democrats and Christian Democrats. He meets privately with Vice-President Bush and Deputy Secretary of State William Clark. In subsequent letter to Vice-President Bush, Archbishop Rivera says the military junta is not "centrist," that the United States military aid is strengthening the hand of the military, and that U.S. military pressure is essential for getting the military to negotiate.	Bush and Clark reject offer.
	Mar.	Secretary of State Haig announces that U.S. economic aid to *Nicaragua*, suspended by President Carter due to alleged flow of arms from Nicaragua to El Salvador, will be resumed when flow stops.	No U.S. aid is forthcoming, even though arms flow is insignificant by April 1981 (according to Lawrence Pezzullo, the U.S. ambassador).
	Aug.	Bilateral exchanges between *Nicaragua* and *U.S.* (August through October). Assistant Secretary of State for Latin America Thomas O. Enders goes to Nicaragua and proposes	Nicaragua says that it is not sending arms to El Salvador and that any arms flow is through illegal activities of private individuals. Nicaragua proposes that U.S. cooperate

Year	Month	Proposal	Response
1981	Aug.	that the U.S. will not support counterrevolutionaries (i.e., *contras*) or isolate Nicaragua economically and diplomatically, if Nicaragua stops supporting Salvadoran insurgents, ends its military buildup, and reduces Cuban military presence.	with intelligence information so Nicaraguan government can stop arms flow. They also stress that a negotiated settlement in El Salvador would be best way to address arms flow issue. Both U.S. and Nicaragua consider each other's proposals insincere.
	Aug.	Mexico and France recognize FMLN-FDR as "representative political force" in *El Salvador* and call for negotiations.	U.S. is very disapproving of political recognition of FDR-FMLN and discourages other U.S. allies from following suit.
	Oct.	Sandinista commander Daniel Ortega reads Salvadoran FDR-FMLN negotiation proposal to the U.N. General Assembly.	U.S. calls proposal "repackaging" of earlier proposals.
1982	Feb.	*Nicaragua* presents peace plan to COPPAL (Permanent Conference on Latin American Political Parties), which is meeting in Managua.	
	Feb.	Soon after Nicaraguan proposal, Mexican President López Portillo presents negotiation proposal regarding both *Nicaragua* and *El Salvador*. Mexico proposes series of nonaggression pacts and demilitarization of Nicaragua. Mexico also asks U.S. to cease force in region and disband *contras* and exiles in training in U.S.	Reagan administration does not support plan, although 100 congressional representatives sign a letter urging President Reagan to accept López Portillo's offer. Nicaragua (and Cuba) agree to accept López Portillo's proposals.
	April	U.S. Ambassador Anthony Quainton in *Nicaragua* presents eight points for discussion with Nicaragua. These points are a restatement of Enders's 1981 proposals with the additional demand that Nicaragua democratize its internal policies (i.e., hold elections).	Nicaragua responds with thirteen-point agenda and agrees to talk about the eight U.S. points but insists on high-level talks to be held in Mexico with Mexicans as moderators. U.S. responds by insisting that talks be at ambassadorial level

Year	Month	Proposal	Response
1982	April		and that Mexico be excluded. In exchange of notes over next several months, Nicaragua agrees to talk about its ties to guerrillas and suggests international verification measures, without U.S. involvement, to insure arms reductions. Nicaragua repeats demand that Mexico be present. U.S. refuses.
	July–Aug.	Salvadoran bishops and Pope John Paul II urge "dialogue" in El Salvador.	
	Sept.	President Herrera Campins (Venezuela) and López Portillo (Mexico) send President Reagan a letter proposing to mediate between *Honduras* and *Nicaragua*.	U.S. ignores proposal and instead organizes a "Peace Forum" in Costa Rica in early October to focus on the contrast between El Salvador and Nicaragua (i.e., elections).
	Oct.	As it launches important military offensive, the FMLN in *El Salvador* calls for "dialogue without preconditions" in a letter delivered to the Salvadoran government and military by Archbishop Rivera y Damas. Letter suggests various sectors of Salvadoran society participate in talks.	Offer rejected by Salvadoran government and U.S. (but even some army officers say it should not be rejected out of hand).
1983	Jan.	Mexico, Venezuela, Colombia, and Panama form *Contadora Group* and begin shuttle diplomacy between governments of region. Initial emphasis is on keeping war from spreading over borders, especially between *Nicaragua* and *Honduras*.	
	Mar.	Pope John Paul II supports "dialogue" in *El Salvador*.	
	May	In order to get congressional approval for Central American military and economic aid,	Stone meets with FDR-FMLN in El Salvador several times. No concrete proposals develop.

Year	Month	Proposal	Response
1983	May	President Reagan appoints ex-Senator Richard Stone as a special envoy to encourage negotiations.	
	July	*Contadora Group* makes detailed proposals for negotiations.	U.S. acknowledges proposals but at the same time dispatches U.S. fleet to patrol both coasts of Nicaragua and announces massive military exercises in Honduras for November.
			Proposal welcomed by Nicaragua (and Cuba).
	July	*Nicaragua* says it will participate in multilateral talks. Up until this point it has pushed for bilateral talks.	
	Sept.	*Contadora Group* proposes Twenty-One Points as a basis for peace in Central America.	Proposal is signed by all five Central American nations. U.S. subscribes in principle.
	Oct.	*Nicaragua* presents four draft treaties, within the Contadora framework. Treaties address relations with U.S. and Honduras and Salvadoran conflict.	U.S. dismisses proposals in less than 24 hours.
	Oct.–Dec.	*Nicaragua* asks Salvadoran insurgent leaders to leave the country, asks some Cubans to leave, eases press censorship, initiates dialogue with Roman Catholic church hierarchy, declares amnesty for Miskito political prisoners and most *contras*, and announces election timetable.	U.S. officials dismiss actions as tokens (or as a sign that pressure is working and should be increased).
1984	Jan.	FMLN in *El Salvador* offers proposal for broad-based provisional government and negotiations between FMLN-FDR and Salvadoran government, army, and the U.S. Specific proposals include formation of new army and police, dismantling of death squads, trial of those re-	U.S. and Salvadoran governments ignore proposal. Duarte (as candidate) calls FMLN proposals "ridiculous."

Year	Month	Proposal	Response
1984	Jan.	sponsible for atrocities, and political reforms, including elections.	
		Kissinger Commission report is released and recommends a combination of military and economic aid. Report also reminds Nicaragua that "force remains an ultimate recourse." Critics of report argue that the report was produced as a justification of U.S. policy in Central America.	
	April	U.S. admits it has been supervising the mining of *Nicaraguan* harbors over the last several months.	Nicaragua protests and takes complaint to International Court of Justice (World Court). U.S. rejects the Court's jurisdiction over its activities in Central America.
	May	In a unanimous vote (416–0), U.S. House of Representatives approves Solarz resolution in support of Contadora process.	
	May	International Court of Justice calls on U.S. to stop the mining of *Nicaragua*'s ports. In interim decision, Court also says that U.S. should not engage in military activities that threaten Nicaraguan sovereignty and political independence.	U.S. focuses on seeking to dismiss case through questions about jurisdiction. U.S. claims it stopped mining harbor previous month.
	May	Mexican President Miguel de la Madrid addresses U.S. Congress and urges U.S. to reject East-West analysis of the conflict. He stresses that change in other countries is not a threat to U.S. security.	
	June	FMLN-FDR in *El Salvador* proposes talks with new government and proposes church act as mediator.	

Year	Month	Proposal	Response
1985	Aug.	U.S. Special Envoy Schlaudeman meets with the deputy foreign minister of *Nicaragua*	For the first time Nicaragua allows "domestic issues" (i.e., Nicaraguan elections) to be discussed at "foreign affairs" talks.
	Sept.	Major *Contadora Group* peace proposal is presented to Central American countries involved in conflict. *Nicaragua* agrees to accept all recommendations, and says it will sign without modifications.	U.S. withdraws its support of Contadora proposal "as is." U.S. implies document needs more details (although all countries have had several months to submit changes).
	Sept.	European foreign ministers and Central American leaders meet in Costa Rica to discuss cooperative economic relations between *Europe* (European Economic Community, Spain, and Portugal) and *Central America*. Europeans give strong support to latest Contadora proposal.	Secretary of State Schultz sends letter urging European ministers not to give aid to Nicaragua.
	Oct.	Contadora ministers, meeting in Panama, express frustration at U.S. efforts to block Contadora proposal.	
	Oct.	President Duarte of *El Salvador* meets with representatives of FDR-FMLN in La Palma.	Both Duarte and FDR-FMLN representatives express willingness to continue talks in November. Fighting soon resumes.
	Nov.	Salvadoran government and FMLN hold second secret meeting.	
1985	Jan.	U.S. suspends bilateral talks with Nicaragua. Dialogue in El Salvador stalls.	
	Feb.	Dispute between Costa Rica and Nicaragua leads Contadora Group to cancel meeting.	
	Feb.	Possibility of negotiated solution seems bleak.	

COUNTRY PROFILES

GUATEMALA

General Data

Area: 42,042 sq. mi. (size of Tennessee).
Population: 7,714,000.
Capital: Guatemala City (approx. 1,000,000).
Geography: Central-western highlands from Guatemala City north (where Indian population lives); broad coastal plain (agroexport area); jungle areas to the north; hills and more arid areas to the east.

Economy

Chief export crops: Coffee, cotton, sugar, bananas, beef.
Chief customers: U.S. (28.6%); EEC (17.4%); Lat. Am. (34.9%).
Gross domestic product: $5.6 billion.
Government expenditures: $1.087 billion.
Foreign debt (May 1983): $2 billion (public and private).
U.S. aid (1984): Military $0
　　　　　　　　　 Economic $35.9 million

Demographic and Social Indicators

Per capita income: $1,140.
Population density: 64.3 inhabitants/sq. km.
Life expectancy: 49 years.
Infant mortality: 76.5/1,000 live births.
Adult literacy rate: 46%.

Despite some mechanisms of formal democracy, the real arbiter in Guatemala since the CIA-sponsored overthrow of the Arbenz government in 1954 has been the army. In March 1982, a military coup overthrew Gen. Romeo Lucas García after his government carried out an electoral fraud in favor of the official candidate. Gen. Efraín Ríos Montt, a "born-again" Christian, was head of government until he was overthrown by Gen. Oscar Humberto

Mejía Victores in August 1983. Throughout this period the Guatemalan army has killed tens of thousands of Indians in the highlands in the name of counterinsurgency and, in the words of the human rights organization Americas Watch, has made Guatemala a "nation of prisoners." The election in 1984 of a constituent assembly ostensibly prepared the way for civilian rule, but there was no doubt that ultimate power would remain with the army.

EL SALVADOR
General Data

Area: 8,260 sq. mi. (size of Massachusetts).
Population: 4,685,000.
Capital: San Salvador (approx. 800,000).
Geography: Flat coastal plains and inland valleys (sugar, cotton, beef), giving way to hills (coffee) that lead to arid mountains in northern part along Honduran border; volcanoes and volcanic soil, no jungles.

Economy

Chief export crops: Coffee, cotton, sugar, beef, shrimp.
Chief customers: U.S. (43.3%); EEC (24.8%); Lat. Am. (22.2%).
Gross domestic product: $3.3 billion.
Government expenditures: $680 million.
Foreign debt (1982): $2.3 billion (public and private).
U.S. aid (1984): Military $196.55 million.
              Economic $47.70 million.

Demographic and Social Indicators

Per capita income: $680.
Population density: 225 inhabitants/sq. km.
Life expectancy: 56 years.
Infant mortality: 78.7/1,000 live births.
Adult literacy rate: 62%.

The military have ruled El Salvador for over fifty years with only two brief episodes of civilian rule, totalling less than a year. A military coup in October 1979 ostensibly ushered in a reform government, which in fact became very repressive. There were several shifts in the junta formula until nominally civilian rule was established by the election of March 1982 for a constituent assembly. Presidential elections in March–May 1984 made Christian Democrat José Napoleón Duarte president, but decisive power remained in the hands of the military and the United States, which was directing and funding the war against the FMLN-FDR, and contributing a large percentage of the Salvadoran government budget.

HONDURAS

General Data

Area: 43,277 sq. mi. (size of Tennessee).
Population: 4,276,000.
Capital: Tegucigalpa (approx. 500,000).
Geography: Mountains occupy most of the western part of the country; broad plains extend to the north (where banana companies operate); the tropical lowlands in the eastern half of the country are almost uninhabited.

Economy

Chief export crops: Bananas, coffee, timber.
Chief customers: U.S. (58.3%); EEC (18.3%); Lat. Am. (11.6%).
Gross domestic product: $2.9 billion.
Government expenditures: $221 million.
Foreign debt: $1.43 billion.
U.S. aid (1984): Military: $191.5 million (not including cost of maneuvers).
                   Economic: $60.1 million.

Demographic and Social Indicators

Per capita income: $640.
Population density: 31.8 inhabitants/sq. km.
Life expectancy: 49 years.
Infant mortality: 76.5/1,000 live births.
Adult literacy rate: 57%

After eighteen years of direct military rule (and several coups) Honduras moved back toward civilian rule by means of elections held in 1980 and 1981. The vote favoring the Liberal party candidate, Roberto Suazo Córdoba, was interpreted as a vote against the army, which had had ties to the National party. Ironically, the role of the army increased because of its importance in U.S. strategy. In particular, Gen. Gustavo Álvarez became the real ruler of the country (in close association with the U.S. ambassador, John Negroponte). The April 1984 coup expelling Álvarez may be seen as an assertion of collective military rule in reaction to Álvarez's personalistic style.

NICARAGUA
General Data

Area: 45,698 sq. mi. (size of Pennsylvania).
Population: 2,954,000.
Capital: Managua (615,000).
Geography: The western half of the country is occupied by low, rugged mountain ranges separated by basins and fertile valleys; a string of about forty volcanoes extends along the Pacific coast; there are two large lakes; the hills in the central part of country give way to sparsely populated tropical lowlands in the eastern half.

Economy

Chief export crops: Coffee, sugar, cotton, timber.
Chief customers: U.S. (26.1%); EEC (16.3%); Lat. Am. (11.2%).
Gross domestic product: $2.4 billion.
Government expenditures: Not available.
Foreign debt: $3.5 billion.
U.S. aid (1984): None.

Demographic and Social Indicators

Per capita income: $897.
Population density: 22 inhabitants/sq. km.
Life expectancy: 55 years.
Infant mortality: 94/1,000 live births.
Adult literacy: 48% before revolution; 88% after literacy campaign.

In July 1979, the forty-five-year Somoza dictatorship was overthrown by a popular insurrection led by the Sandinista National Liberation Front. Formally the executive power was in the hands of a junta and the State Council operated as a kind of assembly, although its members were chosen by sectors instead of by direct representation. Effective power is held by the nine-person Sandinista National Directorate. People participate in government through organizations of workers, peasants, farm laborers, women, youth, professional people, and neighborhood committees. In November 1984, Nicaragua held elections, although a major opposition candidate, Arturo Cruz, after months of negotiation with the Sandinistas, refused to participate. Sandinista commander Daniel Ortega was elected president with 68 percent of the votes cast.

COSTA RICA

General Data

Area: 19,653 sq. mi. (size of New Hampshire and Vermont combined).
Population: 2,624,000.
Capital: San José (approx. 600,000).
Geography: Mountainous; most people have tended to live in the central highlands, farming in the valleys; on the Pacific coast are shallow valleys; on the Atlantic, tropical lowlands.

Economy

Chief export crops: Coffee, bananas, beef, sugar.
Chief customers: U.S. (35.3%); Lat. Am. (34.9%); EEC (26.5%).
Gross domestic product: $5.1 billion.
Government expenditures: $1.218 billion.
Foreign debt: $4.1 billion (public and private).
U.S. aid (1984): Military: $140.1 million
　　　　　　　　 Economic: $52.0 million

Demographic and Social Indicators

Per capita income: $1,520.
Population density: 44 inhabitants/sq. km.
Life expectancy: 68 years.
Infant mortality: 22.3/1,000 live births.
Adult literacy rate: 88%.

Since 1948 Costa Rica has had the most smoothly functioning electoral democracy in Latin America. The lack of an army since the late 1940s and the existence of welfare-state institutions have combined to make the country's standard of living one of the highest in Latin America and relatively equitable. As a result, Costa Ricans are proud of their political system and even conservative in their political behavior—for example, the Communist party functions legally, publishes a daily paper, and can elect representatives to congress but attracts only a small minority. Political parties alternate in power, and elections are scrupulously honest. For example, police power is in the hands of the electoral council and not the president during the pre-election period. Pressures from the United States and its own elites to serve U.S. strategy against Nicaragua, coupled with the country's internal financial and economic crisis, are putting a severe strain on Costa Rica's democratic institutions and its neutrality.

Sources: Mesoamérica (Costa Rica), August 1983, based on data from the World Bank and other international agencies; François Geze et al., eds., *Worldview 1984* (New York: Pantheon Books, 1984); PACCA (Policy Alternatives for the Caribbean and Central America), *Changing Course: Blueprint for Peace in Central America and the Caribbean* (Washington, D.C.: Institute for Policy Studies, 1984); IFCO (Interreligious Foundation for Community Organization), "A Central America Primer."

GLOSSARY OF ACRONYMS AND PROPER NAMES

Álvarez, Enrique Dairy rancher, chosen president of FDR in April 1980 and murdered in November of that year.

Álvarez, General Gustavo Head of Honduran armed forces and most powerful person in the country until overthrown in the April 1984 coup.

ANSESAL Salvadoran National Security Agency, set up with CIA help in the 1960s.

ARENA National Republican Party, set up in El Salvador by Roberto d'Aubuisson and others in preparation for the 1982 election; a political arm of the death squads.

Contadora Group Governments of Mexico, Venezuela, Colombia, and Panama, which pursued negotiations in Central America starting January 1983; named after Panamanian island of Contadora, where they first met formally.

Contras I.e., *contrarevolucionarios* ("counterrevolutionaries"), anti-Sandinista exiles organized into an army with CIA funding and help.

D'Aubuisson, (ex-Major) Roberto Former official in Salvadoran National Guard and ANSESAL; generally believed to be founder of the death squads and involved in the murder of Archbishop Oscar Romero. Leading member of ARENA party and presidential candidate.

Duarte, José Napoleón Leading Christian Democrat of El Salvador; twice mayor of San Salvador; president of the junta December 1980–April 1982; elected president of El Salvador March–May 1984.

ERP Revolutionary People's Army, a guerrilla organization founded in 1970.

FDR Revolutionary Democratic Front, an umbrella political organization of the Salvadoran opposition, set up in April 1980; linked to FMLN.

FECCAS   Federation of Christian Peasants of El Salvador, largest of the "popular organizations." Started by Christian Democrats in early 1960s, it became militant with new leadership in the 1970s, and was eventually linked to the FPL (Popular Liberation Forces), a guerrilla organization.

FMLN   Farabundo Martí National Liberation Front, an umbrella organization of five Salvadoran guerrilla organizations, named after the leader of the aborted 1932 uprising; linked to FDR.

García, General Guillermo   Salvadoran defense minister from October 1979 until forced to retire in April 1983.

Guerra y Guerra, Colonel René   Main leader of reform sector of the Salvadoran military, major organizer of the coup, but soon displaced by more traditional and hard-line officers.

Gutiérrez, Colonel Jaime Abdul   Member of Salvadoran junta starting in October 1979.

Hernández Martínez, Maximiliano   Dictator of El Salvador 1931–44; oversaw 1932 massacre of perhaps 30,000 peasants. A death squad of the 1980s takes its name from Hernández Martínez.

Majano, Colonel Adolfo Arnoldo   Junta member, representative of the reform sector of the military; forced off the junta in December 1980.

ORDEN   Democratic Nationalist Organization, paramilitary network set up, with U.S. help, in El Salvador in the 1960s for spying and intimidation.

Pastora, Edén   Sandinista leader who became famous after co-leading August 1978 action in which 2,000 people were taken hostage in the National Palace. Left the Sandinista government sometime after the fall of Somoza; eventually reappeared, saying he would fight the Sandinistas.

somocismo   "Somoza-ism," i.e., whatever would be a continuation of the Somoza system within Nicaragua.

Walker, William   American adventurer from Tennessee who went to Nicaragua in the 1850s, fought on the Liberal side, became head of the army and even president, with aspirations to make Nicaragua a U.S. state—until he was overthrown by an army from neighboring countries. A symbol of U.S. "imperialism."

REFERENCES

INTRODUCTION

Page 3: Television coverage
Emile G. McAnany, "Television and Crisis: Ten Years of Network News Coverage of Central America," mimeo (College of Communication, University of Texas, January 1982), p. 10. Besides providing interesting quantitative material on what is—and is not—news in Central America, this study shows how television reporting tends to reinforce stereotypes rather than convey a clear sense of events rooted in history.

Page 3: Central America "at our doorstep"
Reagan television address May 9, 1984, reported in *New York Times* May 10, 1984.

Page 4: Statistics on people killed
Figures are imprecise. Forty thousand is the generally accepted figure for the Nicaraguan war, but some Nicaraguans say 50,000. In August 1984, Tutela Legal, the Catholic human rights agency in El Salvador, adjusted its figure for those killed, based on sworn testimony from family members and its own investigations, to 50,000; *Philadelphia Inquirer*, August 24, 1984. Figures for Guatemala are more imprecise. Guatemalan leftists speak of 80,000 people killed. The Committee of the Families of Disappeared Persons accumulated a list of 15,325 cases from 1970 to 1975; Lars Schöultz, "Guatemala: Social Change and Political Conflict," in Martin Diskin, ed., *Trouble in Our Backyard: Central America and the United States in the Eighties* (New York: Pantheon Books, 1983), p. 183. Monitoring Guatemalan daily papers, I documented 1,371 individual political killings in 1979, and certainly many such incidents went unreported.

Page 4: U.S. reconnaissance involvement in Salvadoran war
Washington Post, April 12, 1984.

Page 5: Conservative and liberal frameworks

What began as a trickle of writing when the crisis was first noticed in the late 1970s has now become a torrent. The titles cited here represent only a portion.

Early conservative expressions: James R. Whelan, *Through the Looking Glass: Central America's Crisis* (Washington, D.C.: Council for Hemispheric Security, 1980). See also council booklets on individual countries—e.g., L. Francis Bouchey and Alberto M. Piedra, *Guatemala: A Promise in Peril* (1980) (note that in 1984 Piedra was appointed U.S. ambassador to Guatemala); Roger Fontaine, Cleto DiGiovanni, Jr., and Alexander Kruger, "Castro's Specter," *Washington Quarterly* 3, no. 4 (Autumn 1980); Cleto DiGiovanni, "U.S. Policy and Marxist Threat to Central America," *Heritage Foundation Backgrounder*, October 15, 1980; Constantine Menges, "Central America and Its Enemies," *Commentary*, August 1981. Menges occupies the Latin American desk at the National Security Council, a position earlier held by Fontaine.

Howard J. Wiarda edited a special issue on Central America of the American Enterprise Institute's *Foreign Policy and Defense Review* 4, no. 2 (May 1982).

Early liberal views: Richard Feinberg, "Central America: No Easy Answers," *Foreign Affairs* 59, no. 5 (1981); Robert White, "Central America: The Problem That Won't Go Away," *New York Times Magazine*, July 18, 1982; James Chace, "Getting Out of the Central American Maze," *New York Review of Books*, June 24, 1982; Robert Pastor, "Our Real Interests in Central America, *Atlantic Monthly*, August 1982; Alan Riding, "The Central American Quagmire," *Foreign Affairs* 61, no. 3 (1982).

A symposium in *Foreign Policy* (Summer 1981) presented articles from various perspectives by Leonel Gómez and Bruce Cameron, W. Scott Thompson, J. Bryhan Hehir, Olga Pellecer, and Marlise Simmons.

An excellent collection of analytical overviews is found in Abraham Lowenthal and Samuel Wells, Jr., eds., "The Central American Crisis: Policy Perspectives," mimeo (Washington, D.C.: Latin American Program, Wilson Center, 1982).

The following are collective policy critiques: Martin Diskin, ed., *Trouble in Our Backyard: Central America and the United States in the Eighties* (New York: Pantheon Books, 1983); Richard Feinberg, ed., *Central America: International Dimensions of the Crisis* (New York: Holmes & Meier, 1982); Robert S. Leiken, ed., *Central America: Anatomy of Conflict* (New York: Pergamon Press, 1984); Richard Newfarmer, ed., *From Gunboats to Diplomacy: New U.S. Policies for Latin America* (Baltimore: Johns Hopkins University Press, 1984).

Two collections of Latin (primarily Central) American analyses: *Foro In-*

ternacional (review published by the Colegio de México) 20, no. 4 (April–June 1980); and Trinidad Martínez Tarragó and Mauricio Campillo Illanes, eds., *Centroamérica: Crisis y Política Internacional* (Mexico City: Siglo XXI, 1982).

Penny Lernoux, *Fear and Hope: Toward Political Democracy in Central America* (New York: Field Foundation, 1984), begins by questioning the cultural presuppositions of U.S. policy and goes on to outline an alternative.

A particularly incisive study is Allan Nairn, "Endgame: A Special Report on U.S. Military Strategy in Central America," *NACLA* (North American Congress on Latin America) *Report on the Americas* 18, no. 3 (May–June 1984). Richard Alan White, *The Morass: United States Intervention in Central America* (New York: Harper & Row, 1984), analyzes all of the United States' policy in Central America as essentially an application of counterinsurgency.

The chapter on Central America in *The Americas in 1984: A Year for Decisions—Report on the Inter-American Dialogue* (Washington, D.C.: Aspen Institute for Humanistic Studies, 1984) firmly supports a negotiated approach along the lines of what the Contadora countries propose. This study represents the consensus of a panel of prestigious participants from Latin America and the United States.

Finally, I may cite *Changing Course: Blueprint for Peace in Central America and the Caribbean* (Washington, D.C.: Institute for Policy Studies, 1984). This PACCA (Policy Alternatives for the Caribbean and Central America) report is the product of over a year's work by more than thirty specialists around the United States (including the author); it is based on extensive consultations with representatives from the many church, peace, and labor organizations involved in Central America, and in that sense is a comprehensive alternative proposal to existing policy.

Page 6: Kissinger Commission witness list
"List of Appearances Before the National Bipartisan Commission on Central America in Washington, D.C., August 31–December 12, 1983." An examination of this list shows that almost all the witnesses are business people, bankers, military officers, or representatives of government or private agencies. Almost none have had sustained grassroots experience. Among those who have no special Central America expertise I may cite Arthur Schlesinger, Irving Louis Horowitz, Samuel Huntington, Norman Podhoretz, and Michael Novak. To illustrate another type of selectivity: only 3 of the 104 witnesses were women. In addition to spoken testimony, the commission received well over 200 written testimonies, solicited and unsolicited.

ONE. ORIGINS OF THE CONFLICT

The best single volume on the history of Central America before the outbreak of the present crisis is Ralph Lee Woodward, Jr., *Central America: A Nation Divided* (New York: Oxford University Press, 1976), which includes an extensive annotated bibliography. A Central American view that emphasizes economic development, especially the successive agroexport crops, is Edelberto Torres-Rivas, *Interpretación del Desarrollo Socioeconómico Centroamericano*, 3rd ed. (San José, C.R.: EDUCA, 1973). Walter LeFeber's history *Inevitable Revolutions: The United States in Central America* (New York. W. W. Norton, 1983) provides a great deal of detail, especially on periods prior to the 1970s.

Page 13: U.S. intervention in Honduras
LaFeber, *Inevitable Revolutions*, pp. 42–46.

Page 13: Sandino
Richard Millett, *Guardians of the Dynasty: A History of the U.S.-Created Guardia Nacional de Nicaragua and the Somoza Family* (Maryknoll, N.Y.: Orbis Books, 1977), *passim*, esp. pp. 61–163.

Page 13: 1932 massacre
Thomas Anderson, *Matanza: El Salvador's Communist Revolt of 1932* (Lincoln: University of Nebraska Press, 1971). Anderson finds the commonly accepted figure of 30,000 deaths implausible, and proposes a figure of 10,000.

Page 14: CIA overthrow of Arbenz government
Stephen Schlesinger and Stephen Kinzer, *Bitter Fruit: The Untold Story of the American Coup in Guatemala* (Garden City, N.Y.: Doubleday, 1982); Susanne Jonas and David Tobis, *Guatemala* (Berkeley, Calif.: North American Congress on Latin America, 1974).

Page 16: Agricultural land in Guatemala
Shelton H. Davis and Julie Hodson, *Witnesses to Political Violence in Guatemala: The Suppression of a Rural Development Movement* (Boston: Oxfam-America, 1982), p. 46; United States Agency for International Development, *Small Farmer Improvement* (loan 520–11–190, 520:26), December 1975, p. 12.

Page 16: Landless people in El Salvador
Melvin Burke, "El Sistema de Plantación y la Proletarización del Trabajo

Agrícola en El Salvador," *Estudios Centroamericanos* (San Salvador), no. 335–336 (September–October 1976): 480.

Page 17: Declining living conditions
Two scholars have assembled data from numerous sources to seek common explanatory factors in the insurgencies in Nicaragua, El Salvador, and Guatemala, documenting especially the declining living conditions during the late 1960s and the 1970s, and the absence of insurgency in Honduras and Costa Rica: John Booth, professor of political science at the University of Texas, San Antonio, "Toward Explaining Regional Crisis in Central America: Socioeconomic and Political Roots of Rebellion," mimeo, n.d.; Jan Flora, professor of sociology at Kansas State University, Manhattan, Kansas, "Roots of Insurgency in Central America," mimeo, 1983.

Page 18: Statistics on Guatemala
The figures on income distribution are from the U.S. embassy in Guatemala, *Quarterly Economic Report: Guatemala*, June 1980, p. 4. The figures on coffee producers come from data given me by ANACAFE (Guatemalan Coffee Growers' Association) in 1977, but I no longer have the documentation.

Pages 20–31: Growth of opposition movements and fall of Somoza
Cf. detailed accounts, with a Spanish and English bibliography in Phillip Berryman, *The Religious Roots of Rebellion: Christians in Central American Revolutions* (Maryknoll, N.Y.: Orbis Books, 1984). On El Salvador, cf. Robert Armstrong and Janet Shenk, *El Salvador: The Face of Revolution* (Boston: South End Press, 1982).

Page 21: ORDEN, ANSESAL, *and U.S. involvement*
Allan Nairn, "Behind the Death Squads," *The Progressive*, May 1984, *passim*. The Medrano quotation is on page 21.

TWO. CONFRONTING REVOLUTION: STEP-BY-STEP

Page 34: Closing of CIA *station*
Allan Nairn, "Endgame," *NACLA Report on the Americas* 18, no. 3 (May–June 1984): 22.

Pages 35–36: October 1979 coup
Raymond Bonner, *Weakness and Deceit: U.S. Policy and El Salvador* (New York: Times Books, 1984), provides an excellent inside view of the coup process, especially the role of Guerra y Guerra.

Page 36: Vides quote
Bonner, *Weakness and Deceit*, p. 162.

Pages 39–40: Murder of Archbishop Romero
Craig Pyes, "Who Killed Archbishop Romero?" *The Nation*, October 13, 1984.

Page 39: Noncombatants killed
Socorro Jurídico, Arzobispado de San Salvador, *El Salvador: Del Genocidio de la Junta Militar a la Esperanza de la Lucha Insurreccional* (no place, no date—probably Mexico, 1981), chart p. 9. At the time, Socorro Jurídico was the official human rights agency of the Archdiocese of San Salvador. Its figures are based on formal testimony gathered from family members of those killed and other witnesses.

Page 41: 15,000 killed during Duarte's first term
Richard Alan White, *The Morass: United States Intervention in Central America* (New York: Harper & Row, 1984), table 2, "Extrajudicial Executions in El Salvador of Noncombatant Civilians for Political Reasons," p. 44. White constructed his chart (covering 1979 to mid-1983) from data in Socorro Jurídico materials.

Page 48: Enders in Managua
William Jesse Biddle, "U.S.-Nicaragua Talks: Going Through the Motions," in Center for International Policy, *International Policy Report*, December 1983, pp. 2–4 and *passim*.

Page 49: On ARENA, *death squads, and U.S. connections*
See the excellent investigative reporting of Craig Pyes in a long series in the *Albuquerque Journal*, December 18–22, 1983. Pyes worked with Laurie Beckland, who did a similar series for the *Los Angeles Times*.

Page 49: 1982 election in El Salvador
Bonner, *Weakness and Deceit*, chap. 15, "Elections Sí, Democracy No," pp. 290–321. See also Edward S. Herman and Frank Brodhead, *Demonstration Elections: U.S.-Staged Elections in the Dominican Republic, Vietnam, and El Salvador* (Boston: South End Press, 1984).

Page 50: Hinton speech
Bonner, *Weakness and Deceit*, p. 359.

Page 50: National Security Council memo
"National Security Council Document on Policy in Central America and Cuba," *New York Times*, April 7, 1983.

Page 52: Newsweek *cover story*
November 8, 1982.

Pages 52–53: Edén Pastora Gómez,
For a Sandinista view providing information on Pastora's off-and-on involvement in the anti-Somoza struggle before 1978, see Humberto Ortega, "Analysis of Edén Pastora," in Peter Rosset and John Vandermeer, eds., *The Nicaragua Reader: Documents of a Revolution Under Fire* (New York: Grove Press, 1983), pp. 223–25.

Page 54: Iklé statement
Remarks of the Honorable Fred C. Iklé, undersecretary of defense for policy to Baltimore Council on Foreign Affairs, Monday, September 12, 1983, News Release no. 450–83, Office of Assistant Secretary of Defense for Public Affairs, Washington, D.C., p. 4.

Page 55: Kissinger Commission report
Report of the National Bipartisan Commission on Central America—January 1984. For critiques see: William M. LeoGrande, "Through the Looking Glass: The Kissinger Report on Central America," *World Policy* 1, no. 2; Stuart Holland and Donald Anderson, *Kissinger's Kingdom? A Counter-report on Central America* (Nottingham, Eng.: Russell Press, 1984); Phillip Berryman, "The Kissinger Commission Report: A Critique," appendix 2 in Berryman, *What's Wrong in Central America and What to Do About It* (Philadelphia: American Friends Service Committee, 1984). Holland and Anderson are Labour members of Parliament.

Page 56: CIA funding in election
The *New York Times*, May 12, 1984, reported that the CIA had spent $2.1 million on the election. Of this amount, $960,000 went to the Christian Democrats and $437,000 to the PCN (Party of National Conciliation), formerly the "official" party. As a right-wing party the PCN might have been expected to support ARENA in the runoff election, but it remained neutral. CIA officials admitted that the money had been spent to prevent D'Aubuisson from winning. It should be noted that $2.1 million can have a great impact in a small, poor country like El Salvador.

Page 56: New York Times *story*
April 23, 1984.

Page 57: Gorman's proposal to use AC–130s
"Reagan's Military Buildup," *Newsweek,* March 19, 1984. See also the excellent summary *U.S. Military Intervention in Central America* (May 8, 1984), produced by The Commission on United States–Central American Relations, which summarizes and provides excerpts from over fifty articles from the U.S. press.

Page 59: Americas Watch on Guatemala
Guatemala: A Nation of Prisoners, report issued in January 1984.

THREE. CONFRONTING REVOLUTION: PATTERNS AND ISSUES

Page 62: D'Aubuisson's relation to the CIA
Allan Nairn describes how D'Aubuisson had maintained ties with the CIA since his days in ANSESAL. D'Aubuisson used CIA-supplied material as evidence when he appeared on television in February 1980 to denounce those whom he charged with subversion, such as Mario Zamora (see p. 38). According to Nairn's sources, D'Aubuisson maintained CIA contacts at least until 1981. Allan Nairn, "Behind the Death Squads," *The Progressive,* May 1984. A report issued by the Senate Intelligence Committee in October 1984 seems to contradict Nairn's findings of long-standing connections between the CIA and other U.S. government agencies and those responsible for the Salvadoran death squads. However, the report's main conclusion is that "there is no evidence to support the allegation that elements of the United States have deliberately supported, encouraged or acquiesced in acts of political violence in El Salvador, particularly extreme right-wing death squad activity"; *Philadelphia Inquirer,* September 28, 1984. See also *Los Angeles Times,* October 11, 1984, and *Christian Science Monitor,* October 12, 1984. Nairn's *Progressive* article supplies a great deal of detailed first-person testimony from Salvadorans such as General Medrano himself. What seems undeniable is the existence of long-standing U.S. ties to military figures involved in the murder of civilians. Did the U.S. "intelligence community" know that these people were killers and simply disregard that fact? Or was it unaware of what many ordinary Salvadoran citizens knew?

Page 62: Figures on U.S. military and economic aid
Richard Alan White, *The Morass: United States Intervention in Central America* (New York: Harper & Row, 1984), charts, pp. 237–38; and U.S., Congress, House, *Hearings and Markup Before the Committee on Foreign Affairs*

and Its Subcommittee on Western Hemisphere Affairs, 98th Cong., 2d sess., 1984, "Review of Proposed Economic and Security Assistance Requests for Latin America and the Caribbean, Recommendations of the National Bipartisan Commission on Central America, February 8, 21, 22, 23, and March 1, 1984," p. 84.

Page 63: General Gorman's influence
Robert S. Greenberger, "U.S. General Is Playing a Crucial Role in Setting Central America Policy," *Wall Street Journal*, June 26,1984.

Page 64: Public opinion polls
Dr. William M. LeoGrande has produced a comprehensive summary, *Central America and the Polls: A Study of U.S. Public Opinion Polls on U.S. Foreign Policy Toward El Salvador and Nicaragua under the Reagan Administration* (Washington, D.C.: Washington Office on Latin America, 1984).

Page 66: 80% Sandinista support figure
"I would assume that, like them or not . . . 80% of the population would stand with the Sandinistas"; Allan Nairn, "Endgame," *NACLA Report on the Americas* 18, no. 3 (May–June 1984): 48.

Page 68: Catholic church
See Phillip Berryman, *The Religious Roots of Rebellion: Christians in Central American Revolutions* (Maryknoll, N.Y.: Orbis Books, 1984), chap. 8, "Christians in Sandinista Nicaragua," pp. 226–67, and chaps. 9 to 11, *passim*.

Pages 69–70: Arms flow to El Salvador
Cf. Raymond Bonner, *Weakness and Deceit: U.S. Policy and El Salvador* (New York: Times Books, 1984), pp. 267–69. Allan Nairn reports that a Salvadoran intelligence officer showed him four classified files containing more than 350 pages of documents purportedly captured from guerrillas. While they spoke of contacts in Cuba and Nicaragua "the documents referred . . . to nothing more than minor equipment transactions involving Nicaragua, Cuba, or the Soviet bloc. Most of these concerned specialized gear such as radios. Far more prominent were black-market arms deals in Miami, Texas, and Western Europe. Meetings involving basic political and military decisions were, according to the minutes, attended only by Salvadorans" ("Endgame," p. 33). As a contract employee with the CIA starting in March 1981, David MacMichael was assigned to process evidence on the arms flow. He concluded that the evidence was lacking. Cf. interview in *Sojourners*, August 1984, pp. 19–22. During 1983 the FMLN claimed to have

captured 3,206 rifles, 61 machine guns, 53 grenade launchers, 1 rocket launcher, 11 artillery pieces, and 40 mortars; *Philadelphia Inquirer*, January 3, 1984. A great deal of useful information is to be found in C. G. Jacobsen et al., "Soviet Attitudes Towards Aid to and Contacts with Central American Revolutionaries," photocopy (June 1984). Jacobsen and his colleagues prepared this report for the State Department. Nevertheless, it found Soviet policy generally cautious and, after 1983, increasingly restricted to state-to-state aid to Nicaragua.

Pages 70–72: Death squads and massacres
Bonner, *Weakness and Deceit*, cf. index; Nairn, "Behind the Death Squads," *The Progressive*, May 1984. In both this article and "Endgame," Nairn points to the fact that the Salvadoran system, which U.S. agencies helped design and set up in the 1960s, is based on assassination and terror. He concludes:

> Public and congressional pressures, however, have compelled the administration to voice public criticism of the death squads even as it secretly funnels aid and intelligence to the military and security forces that run them.
>
> U.S. complicity in the dark and brutal work of El Salvador's death squads is not an aberration. Rather, it represents a basic, bipartisan, institutional commitment on the part of six American administrations—a commitment to guard the Salvadoran regime against the prospect that its people might organize in ways unfriendly to that regime or to the United States.

Page 72: Army rationalizations of civilian deaths
The FMLN points out how even those the army regards as *masas* should be regarded as civilians according to the Geneva Conventions. They further note that the army violates the conventions in several ways—for example, by destroying peasants' food and belongings. See Political-Diplomatic Commission of the FMLN-FDR of El Salvador, *Principal Human Rights Violations in the Salvadoran Armed Conflict*, September 1984, pp. 42–43.

Pages 72–74: Land reform
Figure on peasants killed from Jorge Alberto Ruiz Camacho, president of a peasant organization called ACOPAI, which works with the government. "Many have been killed and dirt is stuffed in their mouths as a symbol"; *Philadelphia Inquirer*, May 28, 1982. Figure on evictions from testimony of William C. Doherty, Jr., executive director of the American Institute for Free Labor Development, before the Senate Foreign Relations Committee, August 4, 1983. A *New York Times* story of July 17, 1983, estimated that

one-eighth of the peasants had been evicted from the lands they were working after they had applied for titles. Roy Prosterman, architect of the Land-to-the Tiller program, arrives at the 24 to 29 percent figure by estimating the number of landless agricultural families at 270,000 to 330,000 and the number of beneficiaries at 79,000 families; from a paper, "Land Tenure and Agriculture in Central America" (University of Washington, October 10, 1983). But Prosterman's figure for beneficiaries includes all those who hold *provisional* titles in the Land-to-the-Tiller program—i.e., more than 42,000 families. As of December 1983, only 5,456 *definitive* titles had been given (Doherty testimony, above; and Kissinger Commission report, p. 75).

It cannot be assumed that the 32,000 beneficiaries of Phase I are really better off. Since they have not had sufficient access to credit or technical advice, and since owners often previously liquidated equipment, many are worse off. Only a third of these cooperatives were operating at a profit in 1983; *New York Times*, July 3, 1983. Finally, it should be noted that in late 1983 the Salvadoran Constituent Assembly voted to raise the limit of land that could be owned from 240 acres to 600 acres. Christian Democrats and U.S. embassy officials saw this vote as effectively curtailing further land reform. *New York Times*, December 14, 1983. On the Assembly's moves against the agrarian reform after Duarte's inauguration see *Washington Post*, May 23 and June 29, 1984, and *New York Times*, May 22 and June 30, 1984.

Page 75: Salvadoran budget figure
In recent years the Salvadoran government budget has been somewhat over $800 million, while U.S. aid has been over $300 million per year. Another way of grasping the magnitude of U.S. aid is to note that El Salvador's *total* agroexports—the mainspring of the economy—equaled $564 million in 1983.

Page 76: Nicaraguan election
The Electoral Process in Nicaragua: Domestic and International Influences— The Report of the Latin American Studies Association Delegation to Observe the Nicaraguan General Election of November 4, 1984. The delegation found that "the behavior of U.S. officials during the six months preceding the elections was clearly interventionist, apparently designed to delegitimize the Nicaraguan electoral process by making sure that the FSLN had no externally credible opposition to run against." It concluded that those opposition parties were not excluded from the election, and that if they did not appear on the ballot it was by their own choice. It points out that the Sandinistas had chosen a West European–style proportional representation system that would "maximize representation of opposition parties in the national legislature." Thus opposition parties to the right of the Sandinistas received 29

percent of the valid votes but will get 36.5 percent of the seats in the new National Assembly. The delegation stated that the elections "augur well for the future of political pluralism in Nicaragua," but that the *contra* war and U.S. economic pressures could truncate or reverse that process. The Latin American Studies Association is the professional association of Latin Americanists in the United States.

FOUR. CONFRONTING REVOLUTION: OUTCOMES

Page 89: Decline in Costa Rican living standards
Mesoamérica (San José, C.R.), February 1983, p. 10.

Page 91: Latin American reaction to direct U.S. combat in Central America
It is conceivable that grassroots organizers in other Latin American countries would seize on the symbolism of a U.S. war in Central America. In Brazil and the Dominican Republic, crowds have chanted anti-IMF (International Monetary Fund) slogans during food riots (blaming the IMF's imposed austerity measures for their worsening condition). Organizers might find it convenient to fan popular resentment over a U.S. war against Latin American populations, as they pressured their governments to default instead of saddling the masses of people with debts acquired by elite governments that did nothing for the poor majority. While such an outcome remains quite speculative, its rebound effect would be more threatening to real U.S. interests than anything leftist governments could do in Central America.

Pages 91–93: Costs of a U.S. invasion
Theodore Moran, "The Cost of Alternative U.S. Policies Toward El Salvador: 1984–1989," in Robert S. Leiken, ed., *Central America: Anatomy of Conflict* (New York: Pergamon Press, 1984). Note that Lt. Col. John Buchanan considers 125,000 troops necessary to defeat the Sandinistas: "52,000 Marines on each coast, 12,000 airborne on the west coast, maybe 8,000 on the Caribbean side, and 8,000 Rangers on each coast." He estimates a death toll of 3,000 Americans, and total U.S. casualties of 15,000 to 20,000; "The Objectives and Costs of U.S. Military Operations Against Nicaragua: An Interview with Lt. Col John Buchanan," *Memo Central America*, Commission on United States–Central American Relations (conducted October 15, 1984).

Page 93: El Salto battle
Frank del Olmo, "Is the Salvadoran Army Worth the Costs?" *Los Angeles Times*, December 9, 1984.

FIVE. THE UNITED STATES AND CENTRAL AMERICAN REVOLUTIONS: IS ANY ACCOMMODATION POSSIBLE?

Pages 95–99: Security threats
The summary of arguments is as found in the Kissinger Commission report, pp. 91ff. For a nuanced article by military specialists, see Joseph Cirincione and Leslie C. Hunter, "Military Threats, Actual and Potential," in Robert S. Leiken, ed., *Central America: Anatomy of Conflict* (New York: Pergamon Press, 1984). Hunter works for the U.S. Navy.

Pages 100–104: New economic model
CRIES (Coordenadora Regional de Investigaciones) in Managua has been co-ordinating a vast collaborative effort by several dozen Central American and Caribbean social scientists. From June 6 to 25, 1983, a group met in The Hague with others from Europe and North America to explore the common lines of their research. See *An Alternative Policy for Central America and the Caribbean: Summary and Conclusions* (The Hague, Netherlands: Institute of Social Studies, 1983).

Pages 101–102: Food policy in Nicaragua
Joseph Collins, Frances Moore Lappé, and Nick Allen, *What Difference Could a Revolution Make? Food and Farming in the New Nicaragua* (San Francisco: Institute for Food and Development Policy, 1982).

Page 106: Voting patterns in the United Nations
U.S., Congress, *Report to Congress on Voting Practices in the United Nations, Submitted Pursuant to Public Law 98–151 and Public Law 98–164*, 98th Cong., 2d sess., February 24, 1984.

SIX. WHAT TO DO

Page 110: Bush and Clark rejection of Rivera's peacemaking effort
Bonner, *Weakness and Deceit*, p. 285.

Page 111: Kissinger Commission report quotations
Pp. 105, 106–7, 119.

Page 113: Twenty-One Points
English translation supplied by the Mexican embassy in Washington. (The original repeated "to" before each verb: "To halt . . . To forbid . . ." and so on.) See William Jesse Biddle, "U.S.-Nicaragua Talks: Going Through the Motions," in Center for International Policy, *International Policy Report*,

December 1983. A Center report dated November 1984, "Contadora: A Text for Peace," contains the main sections of the September 1984 drafts, a summary of State Department objections, and a useful analysis.

Page 116: De la Madrid speech
Philadelphia Inquirer, May 17, 1984.

INDEX

159

ABOUT THE AUTHOR

Phillip Berryman was a pastoral worker in a barrio in Panama during 1965–73, the years in which the new liberation theology and pastoral practice in Latin America were taking shape. From 1976 to 1980, as Central American representative for the American Friends Service Committee, he was in a privileged position to observe the deepening crisis in the region. In 1980, he returned from Guatemala to the United States and now lives in Philadelphia with his wife and three daughters, continuing to do research and writing. He is the author of *The Religious Roots of Rebellion* and has published numerous reviews and articles in such journals as *Commonweal*, *America*, and *The National Catholic Reporter*.

OTHER PANTHEON BOOKS
OF RELATED INTEREST

Trouble in Our Backyard:
Central America and the United States in the Eighties

Edited by Martin Diskin, with a Foreword by John Womack, Jr., and
an Afterword by Günter Grass

0-394-71589-6 $9.95 (paperback)
0-394-52295-8 $20.00 (hardcover)

With Friends Like These:
The Americas Watch Report on Human Rights
and U.S. Policy in Latin America

Edited by Cynthia Brown, with a Preface by Jacobo Timerman and an
Introduction by Alfred Stepan

0-394-72949-8 $8.95 (paperback)

These books are available to organizations for special use. For further
information direct your inquiries to Random House, Inc., Special Sales
Dept., 201 East 50th Street, New York, NY 10022 (212–572–2346).